ACCLAIM FOR
CHILD OF DESTINY: THE EDWIN HARPER STORY

"GREAT story. GREAT miracle."

—JACK CUNNINGHAM

Lead Pastor, Bible World Church, Chesapeake, VA

Author, Internationally Known Speaker

"A fantastic spiritual journey...."

—DANIEL L. SCOTT SR

Veteran Missionary, Multicultural Evangelist,

Author, Internationally Known Speaker

"Miraculous victories... spiritual significance...."

—DOUGLAS D. WHITE

Bishop, Abundant Life of Silsbee, Texas

Internationally Known Speaker

"Powerfully moving. Amazing beyond words...."

—DOUG JOSEPH

Lead Pastor, Christian Apostolic Church, Clarksburg, WV

Bestselling Author of The Skyport Chronicles

.

CHILD OF DESTINY

THE EDWIN HARPER STORY

AUTOBIOGRAPHY

WHITESTONE
PUBLISHING
STONEWOOD, WV, USA

Child of Destiny:
The Edwin Harper Story
By Edwin S. Harper

ISBN-10: 1628830085

ISBN-13: 978-1628830088

Library of Congress Control Number: 2014951007

Printed in United States of America.

MEET THE AUTHORS, WATCH VIDEOS & MORE AT
WHITESTONEPUBLISHING.COM
THE SOURCE FOR GREAT CHRISTIAN READING

WHITEST NE
PUBLISHING

CHRISTIAN RESOURCES | INSPIRATIONAL NOVELS | CHILDREN'S BOOKS

I dedicate this book to my wife, Sharon Kay Kitchen Harper, the love of my life. She believed in me when I had nothing to show but a burden and a burning desire to please God. For the last 30 years she insisted that I write. This is the story that, without her, could not have been told. She indeed is the helpmeet that completed me.

Edwin

Table of Contents

Foreword

My first recollection of Edwin Harper was when he walked to a pulpit in Lexington, Kentucky, to preach a state convention. I stood there as a very young preacher, untested by time but unstoppable in passion, and I quickly became enthralled with the articulation and anointing wherewith the speaker began to pour out his soul. Anything but 'random,' the preparation and purpose of Edwin Harper began to bleed through every word, and one had little choice but to be appreciative of the significance his spirit seemed to represent.

Every individual who has ever marked their world with significance has done so with an unwavering view of the path that got them there. In this autobiography, Reverend Edwin Harper peruses both the past and the perceptions that have brought him to the significance his life represents. His pathway, which started from humble beginnings and outside of the revelation of biblical truth he now holds fast, reveals the divine anointing and God's gentle direction that rested upon him from even the earliest years of his life.

The writings of this book allow the reader to follow this unique life through the various ministry milestones, successful pastorates, and the miraculous victories that have been such a part of his life. To read this book is akin to taking your finger and running it along a spiritual atlas to follow the trail of blessings that has led him from obscurity to a lifetime of spiritual significance.

Be prepared to rejoice at the testimonies of undeniable favor shown to both the man and the ministry in this first installment of the life, the loves, and the leadership of Edwin Harper.

> Douglas D. White
> Bishop, Abundant Life of Silsbee

Chapter 1
Legacy of Miracles

"You have maybe two years to live. Go home. Enjoy your wife and little boy," said the doctor, who was a specialist hired by the Union Carbide chemical company. He had been brought in to assess the condition of a male employee who had developed some urinary problems. The year was 1940. Back then Union Carbide spanned the globe. (In later years Dow Chemical absorbed it.) The specialist had confirmed that the man was terminally ill with a disease called Diabetes Insipidus, which was then incurable and considered fatal until 1960. (Today the condition is treatable, but in 1940 the prognosis was utterly hopeless.)

The employee was named James Wesley Harper. He would later become my father. He was dismissed from work, and the company provided him with a disability income. He returned home to his wife, Ruth Cilicia Kirk Harper, and his young son, Wesley Chilton Harper. At that time they lived on Washington Avenue in St. Albans, West Virginia, in a new two-story brick home. Because of his inability to work, he had to sell that home. They moved into a little two-room house behind the home of my mother's father, in Lick Skillet (now Virginia Heights) off Coal River Road.

For years my grandfather had been a faithful saint of God, attending and helping maintain the Jesus Name Apostolic Holiness Church on Rust Street in west St. Albans. Brother Wilbur Chapman, of Huntington, was serving as their pastor while also pastoring the 25th Street Pentecostal Church in Huntington. He came to visit my grandfather, William (Bub) Kirk. My grandfather (Papa/Poppy) asked Brother Chapman to walk out back and pray for my father.

When Brother Chapman entered into the home he started singing, which was his customary practice. Immediately Mom, Dad, and my older brother (who was two years old at that time) were in an Apostolic prayer meeting. After a short while, Papa insisted that Brother Chapman lay hands on my father and pray for God to heal him. I have heard Mom and Dad tell the story many times. The little two-room house began to shake, and a great presence like a cloud entered the room. Instantly my Dad received strength, stood up, and began to dance in the Spirit across the floor. After some time, when the special presence of God diminished, Dad and Mom embraced and declared that he had been healed.

The next day Dad told Mom that he felt like going to work. She packed his lunch, and he went to the main office of Union Carbide in South Charleston and reported for work.

The boss said, "Before you can come back to work you have to be cleared by upper management." Dad went to a Mr. York's office and gave his testimony about the miraculous event that had just taken place. With great skepticism they told Dad that he was just having a good day and that he should just go on back home to rest.

After he left the office, having headed west, back toward St. Albans, Dad found himself in front of the Naval Ordinance Plant. He just turned in, went to the employment office, and applied for a job. The next day he returned for a physical, in which they declared him healthy enough to work. Two days later he joined the carpenter's crew at the Naval Ordinance Plant (NOP) and went to work. Dad knew that while drawing his NOP paycheck he couldn't keep the Union Carbide disability check that arrived at the first of the month. He took the disability check to Mr. York's office to return it.

They asked, "Why are you bringing this back to us?"

Dad explained that he had been healed by God and was now working fulltime at the Naval Ordinance Plant down the road. They wanted to know if the NOP had given Dad a physical. When Dad explained the sequence of events, they told him that if he could pass their exam he could pass Carbide's. At that time they pulled all of Dad's medical records, set up a time for a new exam, and called in the specialist from New York who had given Dad the original, bad diagnosis. After all was said and done, they concluded that indeed God had healed James W. Harper.

My Dad later related to me that I was the son chosen to preach the Gospel before I was even conceived. During the sickness Dad had promised God that if He let him live he would raise a son consecrated to the purpose of preaching the Gospel of Jesus Christ. Nine years later, after the loss of an infant girl and seven miscarriages, I was born on September 18, 1949, in the Thomas Memorial Hospital, South Charleston, WV. At the time we lived on Sam's Fork in Putnam County on a 100-acre farm. The first place I was taken was to the Calvary Apostolic Church on Hurricane Creek Road, Hurricane, West Virginia. The pastor was Reverend Ernest C. Sowards Sr. Although Dad was licensed in the Church of God, Cleveland, Tennessee—a Trinitarian organization—Mom and Dad worshipped at the Oneness church. Dad would often preach the Sunday morning service for Brother Sowards. Dad said he had enough sense to not violate the doctrine of the church with a Trinitarian comment.

Dad had received the Holy Ghost in the Walnut Street Church of God (St. Albans) during a revival in 1937. Mother had received the Holy Ghost in 1933 under Brother Chapman's ministry and had been baptized in February of that year after they chopped the ice open on the Coal River. I was the youngest of three born to James and Ruth Harper. My brother was eleven years older than I. Between Chilton and me there was only the birth of that infant daughter who lived but a couple of days.

In later years I learned from Brother Sowards something of the principles of my Dad. Brother Sowards would tell of a great financial need that he had in his life. Dad sold a piece of property and brought a large sum of money to Brother Sowards in tithing. Brother Sowards told Dad that all tithing went to the pastor.

Brother Sowards reported that my Dad had responded with, "Once I put the tithes in your hands, it is between you and God." Paying the tithes was Dad's part, and managing the House of God was the pastor's part. The amount of that tithe covered his financial need almost to the penny. Brother Sowards said that he knew Dad had a real relationship with God.

After the farm on Sam's Fork sold, we moved to Grant Avenue in St. Albans, West Virginia. I was told that we lived there about a year, and that is where I formed my first memory of life—I can still recall being held up to a window to watch a bulldozer pushing dirt outside of our home. I may have been 18 months old, but the noise and the excitement of that event returns again and again, every time I am around heavy equipment and construction work. There are some spotty intervals after that, but the picture is clearer after Dad sold that place and we moved to the farm he bought us on Spring Branch of Two and Three Quarter Mile Creek, southeast of St. Albans. Today it is Hampshire Drive off Green Valley Drive. There I spent the next ten years of my life and was nurtured in a country setting under the godly influence of Mom and Dad.

Looking back, I count myself incredibly fortunate to have had Mom's father, William H. (Bub) Kirk, alive for the first 22 years of my life. One of my favorite memories of that period on the farm was his arrival every evening. It was always after dark. He came to help me get to sleep. Our ritual was simple. My grandfather, Poppy, would come in, eat a bite, and then gather me up in his arms. He would carry me to my bed and tuck me in. For my third birthday he had bought me a Bible storybook. He would take it down and read the next story in the book. At the conclusion of that story he would always ask me what other Bible story I wanted him to read to me. After that, he would get down on his knees beside my bed and pray over me. He would then ask me to pray for him and our family. I didn't know it, but he was molding me for a lifetime of ministry. I owe my current storytelling skills to those evenings with Poppy, the Bible, and Jesus.

Chapter 2
Just Supposed to Survive

I remember a traumatic afternoon when I was probably four years old. My dad's brother, Frank, lived in one of the tenant houses on the farm. He was a very favorite person to me. He seemed bigger than life because he enjoyed sharing big tales with me, and I always rewarded him with my childish excitement and asked him for more. It was a warm summer day, and I decided that I was going to go over to Uncle Frank's house, a favorite place of escape. From the back porch of the farmhouse I could see Uncle Frank's. I decide that I could make the journey by myself without Dad or my brother, Chilton, as an escort. They had always walked to the front of our home and walked around the barn to the road to get there. From the back porch it just seemed easier to walk a straight line, which would take me through the pasture field between the back of the barn and the orchard. I set out on my journey, climbed through the barbed wire fence, and took a heading straight toward Uncle Frank's. All of a sudden, Uncle Frank was screaming my name and racing across the pasture toward me. When he reached me he roughly grabbed me up, raced down the hill, and dived under the barbed wire fence just as Cleo, our 2000-pound Hereford bull, crashed into the fencing. I never saw the bull coming, but Uncle Frank saw him start toward the little intruder. Without a doubt, I would not be writing this story now as a 65-year-old man had I not had that wonderful Uncle Frank. Before he died, Dad baptized him, and I was praying with him when he received the Holy Ghost.

Looking back I realize that I was just supposed to survive. I suffered being gored by cows, thrown from horses, and run over by them. One day on the north hill, while I was shooting crows, there was an awful commotion at my feet. Somehow the unbelievable happened, as a mountain rattler (a very venomous snake) struck at me and missed. I was so frightened that I forgot I had a firearm in my hand, and I ran all the way to the house, scared out of my wits.

Daddy made it a point to make me aware of the real world that I lived in. I can remember the many times that he would back the old Chevy pick-up truck to the cellar door and load the truck's bed with incredible amounts of canned produce and meat. We would then climb into the truck together and drive to a location along the Kanawha River, across the tracks from then WV Route 17 (now U.S. 35) to a collection of tattered houses and huts, called "Shack Town." He always brought plenty of brown paper sacks (or "pokes" as some folks called them). When we arrived, people of all ages came running to get what they could from Mr. Harper's truck. I was so shocked my first time there because the little 2- and 3-year-olds ran around with no clothing at all.

Whenever Dad would say grace at the table at night, he always said, "Help us help those who don't have." He was molding a lifetime of practices in me.

One day, during my first year of school, around Christmas time, Daddy insisted that we take a ride to meet someone he said that I would never forget. Along the hillside, on the south edge of the very east end of a street called Kanawha Terrace, there were some small houses that you could see from the street. You couldn't drive a car up to them, so we parked and walked down the bank and then up the hill to a little, shambled house, the next-to-the-last one to the east. Sitting in a rocking chair on the narrow front porch was a very old, black gentleman. Thin white hair dotted his almost-bald head. He was dressed in a pair of well-worn bib overalls. With great respect, he shakily stood.

"Oh, no," said Daddy. "You don't have to stand up for us."

"Oh, yes I do," he insisted in a raspy, weak, and aged voice.

Daddy told him I was his baby boy and that he wanted him to tell me about his life.

He told us that he was 105 years of age. He said that he was nine years old when the Civil War began. He related his life as a boy, growing up in a slave's home in the very house he still lived in. I remember the faraway look in his eyes as he recounted the night that his father came home for his mother to bathe his father's back and put oil in the cuts and welts made by the whip of the enforcer of that particular plantation. He told about the day his mother stood in the door and wept as they took his father away because he had been sold to another plantation. He never heard from or saw him again. He related how that he didn't know what to do when "Mr. Lincoln" sent them word that they were free to leave.

He said, "I's didn't have no place to go, and my Mama and me just stayed here and helped my master." That man died the next year after I met him. Daddy took me to the cemetery to bid him farewell.

My days at the farmhouse were delightful. Mother would stand at the kitchen sink, washing dishes and praying aloud. It was like a private church service.

I can still hear her strong, alto voice singing, "All away, All away. King Jesus will roll my burdens away, if to Him I'll pray. He'll open doors for me, doors I'm unable to see. That's how I know King Jesus will roll my burdens away."

Many times in my teen years I would wake up in the middle of the night hearing mother walking the floor calling on the Lord.

One hot summer day, Daddy was out using a mowing scythe so that the hillside behind our house would look clean, trimmed and neat. This was probably at the insistence of Mom. I had just come into the kitchen for a drink of cold Kool-Aid. Suddenly Daddy stumbled into the kitchen telling Mom that he had just been stung by a wasp. His face was red and huge whelps were starting to blotch all over his arms and neck.

Then, almost in hysteria, he began clawing at his shoes saying, "Get them off! My feet are burning up." Mother ran to the phone and called the office of Thomas Blake, M.D.—the physician that had delivered me. She described the malady, and they told her that he was having an allergic reaction and that she needed to get him to the office immediately. What we did not know was that over the years, after dozens of times of being stung by bees while working on the farm, he had become allergic to bee venom and was about to die. We struggled to get him into our '54 Ford sedan. I stood in the back seat behind the passenger's seat and held his head back so he could breathe.

Mother started praying, and I started repeating, over and over, "Jesus, Jesus, Jesus, Jesus..." We prayed all the way to Doc Blake's. When we reached the doctor's office, Mother pulled into Varner's Exxon station, directly across the street. Two men were standing there. I ran to one of them and asked them to help me carry my Daddy in to the doctor. Dad was swelled so badly by then that even though both of them knew him well, no one recognized him. Once in the office, the nurse, Mrs. Meadows, directed them to put Dad in a cubicle and set us down in the next space.

Mother looked at me and said, "I think your Daddy is dead. I'll be brave if you will. Now until they tell us different, let's pray."

I got down on my knees and prayed the only way I knew how. Mother leaned forward and prayed over and over "In the name of Jesus." It seemed like forever but it was only an hour.

Doctor Blake kept saying, "We're doing all we can, Mrs. Harper." All of a sudden we heard Dad groan, and Doctor Blake cried out, "Thank God, he's alive!" When we had first taken him in they had told us there was no pulse. They gave him shots of adrenaline and pumped his chest. Doc would always reference that day, for as long as he practiced, as the day he saw a miracle.

Dad prayed every afternoon from 3:00 PM until 5:00 PM. I think he started the habit because the sun was so hot by midday that he found relief by retreating to the farmhouse, and since he was never given to wasting time he would go to the upstairs window that opened toward the east and redeem the time by praying. Whenever I walked home from school I would always stop underneath that window, sit down, and lean up against the farmhouse to rest, because I knew in a short time he would be calling my name in prayer. I remember one day in particular that I heard him lower his voice, and he sounded as if he was sobbing out his words. Out of concern I decided to ascend the steps to the second floor. Like all 11-year-olds I knew where to step to keep the stairs from squeaking. At the top of the steps I found the door ajar. There I beheld a scene that is forever seared into my mind. Daddy was on his hands and knees, his hair was down in his face, and his tears and mucus were spilling on the floor. There I was introduced to travail.

I always said, "Dad didn't tell me how to pray. He showed me how to pray."

Not all of my life was made up of great spiritual adventures. I had this wonderful pet, a Boston terrier named Sam. He was a gift from a great friend of Dad's, Delbert Whittington. Delbert's son, Steve, grew up in church along with Reverend David Hudson and me. He was the one person that made me believe that God was not really fair. Steve looked like a movie star; I was a skinny weakling. All I needed to do was spend an afternoon with Steve, then pass by a mirror, and the truth was so blatantly obvious. But this story is about Sam, my dog. He was my constant companion. If Dad or Mom would ever find it necessary to give me a dose of hickory tea, they would first need to put Sam into his pen because while they were spanking, me Sam would charge them as though he was going to eat them up.

One day, Sam came dragging into the front yard. Someone had shot him with a shotgun. He was torn up pretty badly. I couldn't believe anyone could harm something that loved me and that I loved so much. About a month after it happened, I was at the mouth of the hollow coming in from school. I overheard Calvin Wilcox bragging how his brother, Earl, had shot that "#%@#" dog of Harper's. Anger swept over me. I slipped away into the woods and took a shortcut home.

I went into the house, straight to the gun closet, and got my 20-gauge shotgun. I went out across the road upon the north hillside and wound my way around the hill. I sat down about forty yards into the brush behind Earl Wilcox's back door. I sat there as quiet as if I was squirrel hunting, waiting to settle the score with the man who had crippled my pet. In the meantime Dad had come in. He asked Mom if she had seen me.

Mom said, "Oh, he came in a while ago and went back out. I think he's out at the barn."

Dad checked and found I wasn't out there. He then checked the gun closet and saw that my shotgun was missing. Dad could slip through the woods and never make a sound. His mother was a Sioux Indian. I was poised and ready for Earl, when suddenly Dad's hand was on my shoulder as he said, "Don't you think we need to take this gun back to the house?" About that time Earl came out his back door. Ten more seconds and my life would have been ruined forever. Earl would have probably died. Our family would have been shamed. I thank God for a praying father that was in touch with my world.

Chapter 3
Birthright of Truth

Dad had deep convictions about scriptural order. After moving to the farm on Spring Branch, Mother and Dad started worshipping at the Jesus Name Apostolic Holiness Church on Rust Street in west St. Albans. At that time a very colorful and dynamic character, the Reverend Otho Smalley, pastored the church. Due to hard times the church had previously been closed for a couple of years. Brother Smalley, who was the pastor of the Apostolic Church in the Kanawha City section of Charleston, conferred with my grandfather, "Bub" Kirk, and reopened the church in the late 40's. One of the main helpers was a young Daniel Coleman, a zealous Pentecostal (then only 16 years old). He would grow up to build a great church in Tornado, West Virginia, and be a key person in the West Virginia District as a presbyter and holder of several district offices.

On a Sunday afternoon, Dad stopped by Brother Smalley's house to talk to him about a doctrinal question. Dad was a Trinitarian, and Brother Smalley was a One-God Apostolic. No one answered the knock at the front door, so Dad walked around back and found him slumped, sitting on the basement stairway, dead. After the shock of the passing, the church in St. Albans, at which Dad and Mom had no voting voice, elected Sister Macy McDade as pastor. Because Dad said that it was impossible for a woman to be the husband of one wife (a reference to I Timothy 3:2), he and mother started attending the First Pentecostal Church on Patrick Street in Charleston, where Reverend D. W. Durst was the pastor.

One Sunday, Brother D. W. Durst and Sister Pearl Durst and family accepted our invitation to the farm for Sunday dinner. After dinner was finished, Daddy and Brother Durst went to the living room— that one room in the house in which I was not allowed to play—and spent the next several hours talking Bible. I have always suspected that it was regarding the subject Dad went to Brother Smalley's home to discuss the day that he found him dead. Dad and Brother Durst emerged from the shelter of the living room (or front room, as they often called it) with expressions of piety on their faces. Mom later told of Dad coming into the kitchen that day (soon after the Durst family departed to go back to Charleston) with his Bible and reading to her I Corinthians 10:13, "Is Christ divided, was Paul crucified for you or were you baptized in the name of Paul?"

Dad then said, "Seems to me that one ought to be baptized in the name of the One who died for you." As she relayed it, that was all he had to say. All of us got ready to go to church. In service that night they conducted an open testimony service. Dad stood to speak, which was not uncommon, but what he said changed all of our lives.

Dad testified, "I really enjoyed the day with Brother Durst and his family. I thank God for such a loving and kind pastor. Tonight I want to tell all of you something that my wife and babies don't yet know. I am ready to be baptized in the name of the Lord Jesus Christ."

With that a shout erupted because that "Trinitarian" preacher was ready to accept the revelation of the Oneness of God and the name of the Lord Jesus Christ. Brother Kincaid rushed downstairs to fill the baptistery. Kermit, Brother Durst's son, rushed to their nearby house to get a change of clothes. (That was before we knew about baptismal robes.) Glenn and Eva (Brother Durst's son and daughter-in-law) started singing with all of their hearts. When the joy settled, Brother Durst preached. By then the baptistery was full, and this little boy (then three years old) saw his father baptized in the name of the Lord Jesus Christ.

Soon after that, Dad became the Sunday School Superintendent of First Pentecostal Church on Patrick Street. In the next three years the Sunday school reached an attendance of 200 people, and great revival was enjoyed in the church. It was there that I took part in my first public presentation as the open voice at a Christmas play:

I loudly declared, "They told me to say it, and say it loud so you could hear. So, welcome good people. We're glad that you're here."

Meanwhile at St. Albans, Sister McDade resigned as pastor, and she moved to Hometown, WV, where she pastored until her death. The St. Albans congregation asked Brother O'Garry to serve as their pastor. With that, Dad felt comfortable to move his membership back to that church. It was there that my hunger to work for God was really honed. The Sunday School began to grow, and the congregation was outgrowing the building on Rust Street. Names like Leonard Blankenship, Aaron Loudermilk, Delbert Whittington, William H. Kirk, Edgar Harrah and Lola Fridley, Grandma Hall and Adkins, Evie Croasins, Billy Joe and Barbara Sowards speak of those who would help mold me forever. It was there on a Sunday night that my uncle, Reverend Roy Hall, was preaching. I was six years old. I remember the aching fear of missing the rapture. That night I went to the altar for my first time. The next Sunday I probably received the Holy Ghost. (Looking back, I remembered all of the funny words I said). In those days no one would think of saying, "That's the Holy Ghost." It was not until later, when I was 11 years old, that I claimed the victory.

When the church started to talk about constructing a new building in a new location, Brother O'Garry decided to resign as pastor and move on. The members turned to Dad to help them. Dad declared that he was not available to pastor but that he would do all he could to help with the process. He called Brother Durst, who was the presbyter for that section of the East Central District of the United Pentecostal Church, and shared with him the need for a pastor.

Without a pastor the church moved along and located property at 216 Alameda Street in Saint Albans. I remember when the bulldozers came, digging the basement and footers. I remember the laying of block and pouring of concrete. (Dad worked 36 hours straight, then came home and fell asleep in the living room floor.) I remember the day they were raising money for the forced air furnace. Leonard Blankenship, a man with a great story of salvation, pulled a $100.00 bill out of his wallet and challenged everyone to chip in. And chip in they did. They installed the subflooring of the main floor, went on up with the blocks, and then put the roof on the building. It was there that I first learned to work on church buildings. The folks majored on getting the basement ready so they could start worshipping there.

Brother Durst had identified Reverend Maurice Stringer as a likely candidate for the church's pastor. After he was elected, Dad continued to preach until Brother Stringer was able to move to Saint Albans. I remember the night Dad was gone all day helping the Stringer family move. I had an attack of what later turned out to be appendicitis. I remember being awake all night and crying so hard that I vomited. Finally Mom laid her hands on me and began to plead the blood of Jesus. I fell asleep, and the sun was shining the next day when I awoke.

Chapter 4
Destiny Awakened

While we still lived at the farm, I recall a summer day when I was sitting on the long front porch of the old farmhouse. It was like I was having a conversation with an invisible person. I thought, "If I get the Holy Ghost this year, then I will be able to get baptized, read the Bible through, and start preaching in a couple of years." I knew enough about the United Pentecostal Church by then that I reminded myself that I would have to be 17 years of age to apply for Local License. I remember leaving the porch, walking around to the back of the house to the tall stump of a tree that Dad had cut down the year before. There for a little bit I pretended that I was preaching. It didn't last long, and what I said was not very impacting, because I can't remember the message. I am sure it was about Jesus loving me though. I don't recall entertaining the thought again until a remarkable afternoon in 1962.

The following year we worked so hard to have the upstairs ready for Easter morning. Reverend Willard

Blankenship, the pastor of the Gallipolis, Ohio Apostolic Church, finished the hardwood floors. As of that time we still had the old, homemade, slat-backed and slat-bottomed benches that had been in the Rust Street location. We desperately wanted to have 100 in attendance on Easter morning. The count came to 98, and so my mother went outside on the street and gave three boys $2.00 each to come in and be present.

Two of the boys were wearing jeans and t-shirts, and the third said, "My Mom will kill me if she finds out I wore shorts to church." His mother did not kill him. Instead, she came to church with him the next week, and she became a regular at the church.

The church continued to reach people. The revival continued. In May of 1961 I received the baptism of the Holy Ghost, and Pastor Maurice Stringer baptized me in water in the name of the Lord Jesus Christ. I started the seventh grade as a one-God, Apostolic, tongue-talking, Holy Ghost-filled believer in the liberating power of Jesus name. My now life-long friend, Larry Harkins, was greatly moved knowing that his friend had actually received the baptism of the Holy Ghost.

Larry asked me a hundred questions that I, as a new convert, could only answer by saying, "Just go to the altar, ask God to forgive you, and then start calling the name of Jesus over and over." The next Sunday night he, too, received the baptism of the Spirit.

The youth group continued to grow. Our youth leader, Keith Reynolds, was a young graduate of Apostolic Bible Institute. He took particular interest in Larry and me because we were learning to play the trumpet, which Keith played also. Together we performed a trio song titled "Search Me." Every Saturday we would gather and go to a nearby neighborhood to knock doors. This vaccinated me with a lifelong desire to evangelize and get people to church.

After I received the Holy Ghost, there came a fateful summer day while Dad was building us a new home on Kanawha Terrace. We were living in a rented house on Adams Avenue in St. Albans. I was riding my new Huffy bike that I had received for my birthday the year before. About a block from the house I heard mother call my name. I turned around, went straight to the house, and asked her what she needed. She smiled and said that I must be mistaken because she hadn't called for me. I started back out on my trip and about the same location I heard her again. So I turned back to her a second time. When I told her I had heard her call, she sat me down and relayed the Bible story about Samuel and Eli.

She said, "If you hear it again, stop and say, 'Yes,

Lord, your servant heareth.'" I heard, and I answered as I was instructed. I shall never forget the incredible presence that swept over me. Today, I could take you to that spot on Adams Avenue in Saint Albans and show you where I sat down on the curb and wept for 20 minutes. I was overwhelmed that the Lord had called my name.

During this period of time I developed an insatiable desire to learn the Word of God. By the age of 13 I had read the Bible through three times. In that timeframe several things happened that helped me as a young man developing into a stronger Christian. I didn't understand then, but later I learned the details that probably aren't important enough to discuss. However, it began as hurt feelings and ended up that Dad said it would be an abomination to sow discord in a local church body. As a result, for about a year the family went back to the First Pentecostal Church in Charleston.

After months of counseling with Rev. Durst, Dad came to my bedroom one night and said, "Edwin, what would you say if I told you that God has spoken to me and told me to take your college fund and build a church in Nitro, West Virginia?" This was my first encounter with submission and spiritual authority that directly affected my world. Question: how do you tell the spiritual authority in your life no, and how do you tell God no?

This was not a pleasant thought, because my education and college had always been a big deal. The reason was none of our family or blood cousins had any education. We were all farm and country people. I felt the call of God, but I was also very taken with music. This would continue to be the battleground of my soul and mind throughout my secondary education experience. In high school the chorus, band, orchestra, drama, and music theory classes dominated my thoughts. Five of my classmates ended up as professional musicians. Some were ranked below me; two above me. I had won, and would win, several all-state honors and regional awards. I wrote an orchestra piece and directed the high school band in competition and won a scholarship. Yet learning submission early on would eventually settle the *score* once and for all. As much as I admired Leonard Bernstein, the Apostolic ministers around me took top billing in my life.

The First United Pentecostal Church in Nitro taught me the sacrifice and struggles of being a real Apostolic. The years before Nitro were years of learning carpenter work. I especially remember the day Dad left me alone in a bedroom of a house he was finishing. He told me to hang the closet door. I had seen Dad do it many times. That day, at age 13, was my moment to figure out how the job was really done. I tried to remember the sequence that Dad followed. Measuring, building the frame, mortising the hinges, cutting the trim, stops and lock holes—it all seemed a little overwhelming. The problem was that the door wouldn't shut. It will always standout to me how patient Dad was. It cost him a door, but we took it completely apart and did it over. From then on I could hang and finish a door as well as the rest. Oh, the wonder of a pre-hung door.

I related that story because when we started the Nitro church at 315 Frederick Street, I was a main player in the whole project. Some say they worked on the church from the ground up. My work started below the ground, digging the footers and squaring up the dig with a square-tipped shovel. I was able to be a part of every phase of the project, all the way up to the ridge cap.

We bought the pews out of a very pretty Nazarene Church in Cross Lanes, West Virginia. Dad really liked the interior of the building. So I sat down in the corner and sketched out the beam trim in front of the pulpit, the choir area, and the altar space. If you have ever attended the Nitro church, you have seen the finished work.

Drawing from the training of Reverend Keith

Reynolds, I began my personal campaign to knock every door in the city. I called upon a tremendous mentor and influence in my life, Reverend Daniel Scott, our district's Pentecostal Conquerors president and pastor of the Open Door Church on Quarrier Street in Charleston, and asked him to help me print some tracts and handouts for me to use on the street. I can honestly report that I knocked every door in Nitro, West Virginia, before I graduated from high school.

One Sunday, a missionary named Sam Latta came to us. He was on his way to Liberia, West Africa. Dad was so thrilled with him that he insisted that Brother Latta stay and preach a revival. Brother Latta's schedule would not allow that to happen; however, he helped arrange for Reverend James Lashley to come a few weeks later. It only made sense to knock doors again. Brother Lashley will tell you that in all of his evangelizing, I was the only teenage boy to drag him from street to street, and from house to house, door knocking.

He and I have laughed many times over the years about one house in particular. We knocked on the door. A little girl came to the door. We asked if we could speak to the parent.

The girl said, "Sure," and she proceeded to lead us around the corner of the house into the backyard.

Brother Lashley led the way.

As soon as he rounded the corner, Brother Lashley spun around and frantically said, "Brother Edwin, we've got to go back around front." The mother was sunbathing in the nude. We left the tract with the little girl and went on quickly.

Soul after soul was touched in that meeting. Today, several of the young people that were converted in that time frame are now senior citizens attending Apostolic churches.

My father had a very outgoing personality, and he was greatly loved. We made friends with the Nitro City Manager, Richard Barrickman. He received the Holy Ghost with his head resting in my teenage lap.

Speaking of my father's "loving ways," one Fourth of July season some neighborhood boys were setting off firecrackers right outside the church during service. Dad stepped outside, and I followed. I thought sure he was going to really straighten them out, like he would have done me.

Instead, my Dad said, "Gee, fellows, that looks fun. Could I light one?"

"Sure," Clyde Carter said.

Dad lit one and threw it, and then he said, "Boys, if you'll wait until church is over, I'll go get you some more and we'll have some great fun." The noise stopped, and after church Dad kept his word. He ended up baptizing all four of the guys.

Chapter 5
Indelible Imprint

In 1963, after we started the church, I went to church camp during the first year that the East Central District operated the campground at Point Pleasant, West Virginia. One of the great marks in my ministerial life happened that year as Reverend Daniel Scott taught from a big chart about the Tabernacle Plan. He helped shape my understanding of how the Old Testament is a schoolmaster to bring us to Christ. The types and shadows explained the plan of salvation so clearly. It gave me an even greater hunger for the word of God.

I often attended during the first week of camp as a potato peeler and dishwasher in the kitchen just to be in the night services. The second week I would be a camper. My second year at the camp, during a morning service that turned into a mass altar session that put the whole camp roster on its face for the entire time, I saw the Lord in a vision while I was down at the altar on my knees in the sawdust. I saw all of Him but His face. It was a blinding light I could not look into. There I accepted my call to preach the gospel. Brother Danny Scott, our Conquerors president at that time, later told me he has an 8mm movie of that day with me at the altar.

The next Sunday night, Dad came into my room and said that the Lord had revealed to him that something special had happened to me at camp and asked if I would care to share it with him. I told of my visitation with Jesus and my surrender to Him to carry the gospel. He told me to prepare to speak in the next church service. That was August 18, 1964. I have preached on a regular basis ever since.

My father was a spiritual man. Mother was a woman of Scripture and insisted on Bible principles.

"Take a lower seat until you are called up higher. A man's gifts will make room for him. The steps of a good man are ordered of the Lord. Rebuke not an elder, but entreat him as a father." On and on, she drilled into me that I was just a born again child of God, and when my time came God would place me in the body where He saw fit. "Be not weary in well doing, for in due season you shall reap if you faint not." The word of the Lord has never failed me.

I preached revivals while I was still in high school. In fact, my mother drove me to meeting after meeting. My first protracted meeting was for Pastor Dewitt Keyser at the Marmet Apostolic Church. The meeting lasted for two weeks. The first three nights no one came to the altar, but then there was one, then two, and by the end of the meeting several had received the Holy Ghost. The last night there were 13 in the altar. My pay for two weeks work was $5.00 and a new white shirt. Things would get better. Because I was so thin I didn't make a big first impression. If anything came of my preaching, it wasn't looks or personal presence; it had to be the anointing of God.

In my senior year when I was able to drive, during my last semester I only had class for half of the day. For extra credits through a Life Skills training class, I took a job at a service station where I went to work at 2:00 PM. I had a key to the church, so every day between school and work I would go to the church and pray for an hour. I shall never forget this incredible time. I was on my knees for what seemed like just a few minutes when I thought I heard a door open way down a long, hollow hallway. Footsteps echoed. It sounded as if someone was walking toward me. I suddenly realized that somebody or something was standing directly behind me. I must honestly say I was so very frightened. Immediately I felt the weight of a hand rest on my left shoulder. A tremendous calm swept over me as that being began to speak.

"Edwin, the Lord has called you. Today, I come

to tell you that you are a chosen vessel. Think not what you shall say in the hours that you are called upon. I have touched your mind and your heart so that your mouth will be filled with my words. You shall stand before great men of this world and declare the truth of the Lord Jesus Christ. Fear not, for I am with you, saith the LORD. Thousands of thousands will believe at the witness that you give of the LORD. You shall see the world and be instrumental in the spreading of this *message* of *truth*. You must remain humble because none of your future is of your doing. I AM the LORD, and I send you forth into the harvest. Remember always that your steps are ordered of the LORD. Be thou faithful and faint not, for to whom much is given, much is required. I am with you today, and I will be with you when you feel you are least able to fulfill this *call* and *command*."

With that I felt the hand remove from my shoulder. I could sense movement, and then I heard the footsteps going back down or up that hallway away from me. I heard that door close. Too scared to move, I began to sob. When I regained my composure, I was shocked to realize that I was very late for work. Nobody was going to believe this, so I hid it in my heart for some time. Then I got the courage to tell Mom and Dad.

Dad had this calm answer, simply saying, "So is

the work of the Lord." It was never mentioned again.

At Easter during my senior year, Brother Ron Turner, then of Cleveland, Texas, came to preach a revival for us at Nitro. He was fresh from Texas Bible College. Most West Virginians had chosen to go to Bible college in St. Paul, MN. I had always thought that I would follow suit. Yet after spending the month with Brother Turner, I was convinced that being exposed to fifty churches in the Houston area was a better opportunity of education and experience than that of one church in St. Paul. Eventually I made my application, and I was delighted to be accepted.

I would not be going to Houston alone. I was going to take the love of my life with me. I guess it has to be said that God has a plan if we will just follow. It's time to backtrack in the story a little bit.

Way back in July of 1962 I attended a special youth and fellowship rally at the Open Door Apostolic Church on Quarrier Street in Charleston, WV. It has been mentioned that Reverend Daniel L. Scott was pastor there. That night the guest speaker was Reverend Greene Kitchen, the pastor of our district's largest church, the Staunton Street Apostolic Church in Huntington. During his opening remarks he mentioned that he had just concluded a two-week revival in Fayetteville, West Virginia with Pastor Mark

Goodin. Brother Kitchen said that he would like for his evangelistic team to stand with him. The evangelistic team was his 12-year-old daughter, Sharon. When she stood up—she took my breath. I was sitting where I always sat in church, and that was at my mother's side. No fooling around for me.

I whispered to my mother, "How old is she?"

"About your age," she replied.

"When I grow up," I answered, "I'm going to marry her." Nothing else was said or done until 1965.

During the third year of camp at the Point Pleasant site, in 1965, Sharon was again helping her father. Her steady boyfriend of the two previous years, from their home church, had joined the U.S. Navy and had sailed off to San Francisco. Sharon was, to say the least, heartbroken. As most have learned, young love is sometimes painful and at the same time provides seasons of maturing that pave the way for a better future. There happened to be another pastor's son—me.

In fact when she saw me coming across the grounds, she asked a mutual friend, David Hudson, "Who is that skinny guy over there?" I was working at the kitchen that year, so as to be able to spend two weeks at the camp. Far from suave, dressed in blue jeans and a white t-shirt, I worked the pop stand every day and peeled potatoes every evening, helping the cooks prepare the evening meal and after-church snacks. I was probably not as handsome as some of the others, and I probably lacked a considerable amount of social skills, a farm boy simply in love with God and searching for the future. Inevitably Sharon, with her craving for Nehi brand orange soda, spent every break ordering a pop from me, that skinny soda jerk. After a week of conversation I grew to look forward to her next thirsty moment. By the end of the week, like every other boy in the district, I was awestruck with her. Strangely, my unassuming attitude about living for God had become a magnet to the godly heart of Sharon.

Since I had a girlfriend that would be coming to the camp that next week, I thought it wise to tell Sharon that I was "going steady." (I had been going steady for all of one week, and that was while I at camp, away from the girlfriend.) When I informed Sharon of this, she responded that her boyfriend was in San Francisco in the Navy and that she didn't know what to do.

The first day of the next week of camp, Sharon met the "girlfriend," who related to her that Edwin was going to be a "preacher." Sharon felt that, because of having been raised in a pastor's home and witnessing the labor, pressure, disappointments and struggles that the man of God and his family face, the idea of spending the rest of her life in a glass house and raising her children as preacher's kids did not appeal to her at all. However, she was the child that God had used to direct her father's life course. The sovereign will of God was always at the foundation of her commitment to God. After determining that she would enjoy the week and go on, Sharon continued to be very kind to me. I informed a friend of mine that the idea of romance wasn't good for me at that time. Nevertheless, by the end of the week we were totally crippled toward the need to be in each other's presence. Sharon went home and began asking God to take away the feelings that she had for me. In her prayers she told the Lord, "You know, God, that I don't know if I can live under the pressure that my mother and father have lived with."

Whatever the suffering was that her parents had faced, it had invoked a resolute determination not only in her but also in her sister, Charlotte Ann, and in her brother, David Lee, not to be involved with the ministry. Mind you both of her siblings had worked diligently in the local church alongside their parents, but they without question had by-passed and rejected any thoughts at all of following in the vocational footsteps of ministry. Reflectively, some nine years later when Sharon would be the pastor's wife in the Midwest while going through a great deal of pastoral church struggle, she commented she would not have had to face the challenges of this setting if her older sister had married the preacher (a former pastor of the very church Sharon and I were serving then) who had fallen deeply in love with Charlotte— and she had refused his proposal for marriage because she did not want a life in the parsonage. Then David, in spite of the fact that he was a gifted speaker and a favorite of the local congregation, made adamant refusals to become a minister. At any mention of one of his three sons becoming a part of the ministry, he would explain again and again how holy and sacred the office was, and he without fail purposefully discouraged any such consideration in their lives. David, Charlotte, and their children have remained faithful to attendance and support of the church throughout their lives.

Sharon, though, was true to her devotion to God. When the overwhelming desire to have lasting company with me continued she simply resigned herself to say to the Lord, "Not my will, but Thy will be done." At that point great peace came to her. A few days later she started penning a letter that would change her life forever, addressed to the young man in the Navy. Sharon and I were more than a boyfriend and girlfriend. We melted together like butter and became best friends. Later on in life we would comment, "How lucky do you get to marry your best friend?" During one of the Bible classes being taught at camp by Rev. Porter, from Wellsburg, West Virginia, he called on Sharon to lead in prayer to dismiss the class. As bubbly as Sharon was, whenever she was put on the spot she was often very intimidated. She did know how to respond. I was sitting beside her, so she quickly elbowed me for help. I just started out, "Our dear Heavenly Father..." and prayed the prayer for her. In fact, on the last night of the next year's camp, beside the pop stand, I proposed to her.

In November, one Thursday night, I went down to Huntington to enjoy a youth service at Sharon's home church. I did not realize I would be given one of the greatest compliments that I would ever receive. From the platform, her father recognized me as a young minister. I didn't know it, but Sharon had such a respect for the ministry that she could hardly accept the fact that a person as young as me could really be called to preach. Yet when her father called on me to testify and recognized me as a minister, her overwhelming respect for her father's opinion helped persuade her.

She said, "When Daddy called him a preacher—then I knew it was so." Two weeks later I was invited back as the guest speaker for the Tuesday night service.

The following February I was visiting the Open Door Apostolic Church in Charleston. They were in a revival with Sister Willie Johnson. I don't ever remember a person so intense in the demonstration of the anointing of the Holy Ghost and the operation of the gifts of the Spirit. In the course of her ministering, she spun around toward me. I was on the platform, where Brother Scott had instructed me to sit. She swirled her cape over me, laid both hands on my head, and started speaking in tongues.

Then in English she said, "The Lord has called you. Today I come to tell you that you are a chosen vessel. Think not what you shall say in the hours that you are called upon. I have touched your mind and your heart so that your mouth will be filled with my words. You shall stand before great men of this world and declare the truth of the Lord Jesus Christ. Fear not, for I am with you saith the LORD. Thousands of thousands will believe at the witness that you give of the LORD. You shall see the world and be instrumental in the spreading of this *message* of *truth*. You must remain humble because none of your future is of your doing. I AM the LORD and I send you forth into the harvest. Remember always that your steps are ordered of the LORD. Be thou faithful and faint not, for to whom much is given much is required. I am with you today and I will be with you when you feel you are least able to fulfill this *call* and *command*." This would not be the last time I would encounter her insight into my life.

During my senior year of high school at a "Youth for Christ" club meeting, a discussion developed following a young person's testimony about being baptized. I asked if they had been baptized in the name of the Lord Jesus Christ. One comment after another finally provoked a classmate, Norman, to tell me that if I would go home with him tomorrow after school that his father would explain things to me, since I didn't know anything about the Trinity. When I got to the home, his father, the minister at the largest Church of Christ in our area, met me at the door. He started out by asking me if I had ever read the Bible. I assured him that I had not only read it but had memorized long passages of scripture. He told me that I needed instructions about the "God-head." He began by asking me what I knew about the subject. I started in Isaiah and walked from Deuter-onomy, to Psalms, and eventually through the New Testament.

Every time he interrupted me I said, "Excuse me, but I'm not finished." Eventually, I explained I had to go because I had to be at work. The next day, his son told me that if he could, he would like to be baptized in the name of the Lord Jesus Christ. He let me know that his father was stumped. He said that when he had left for school, his father had a lot of books out on the dining room table. He said that when he asked his father what he was doing, his father had replied, "Your friend knows what he is talking about. I don't know how to honestly answer him." I was never invited back.

Chapter 6
A Time For Love

I had continued to work at that gas station, and I preached several meetings. I had come up with enough money to buy Sharon a one-third carat solitaire engagement ring. (It was so small that some of her friends made fun of it.) I finally mustered enough courage to take the ring to her and to formally ask Brother Kitchen for the hand of his daughter in marriage. I remember it well. On March 31, 1967 I went to the Kitchen home, knocked on the door, and was welcomed in by Brother Kitchen.

I took a deep breath and went straight to the point, "Brother Kitchen, I want to tell you that Sharon and I love each other. I love your daughter with all of my heart—so much so that I want to marry her, and I want to ask for the hand of your daughter in marriage."

"Wellllllllll," he said. That was his standard "time buyer" to gather his thoughts as to what he wanted to say. "You know that I have already given Charlotte Ann in marriage. David Lee has taken a wife, and he is gone. Sharon is all I have left." That was his pre-amble. For almost an hour he talked without stopping about Sharon and her virtues, while I squirmed waiting for a final, resounding yes. Charlotte was coming to the house to pick up something from her mother. She found Sharon standing nervously outside the front door of the home.

"What are you doing standing out here in the cold, Sherry?" she asked.

"Oh, Sissy, Edwin is in there asking Daddy if we can get married."

"How long has it been?" asked Charlotte.

"About an hour," Sharon replied.

"Good Lord. Tommy and I just told him we were getting married."

"Really? OK then, I am going in. Edwin's suffered enough." Then the door opened, and Sharon and her older sister came in and interrupted the process. The answer was more or less assumed; I don't really remember him giving a formal yes, but that night they started planning a wedding.

By the next spring conference, I had preached enough to qualify for my initial ministerial credentials, which is formally called "local license." The East Central District Conference would be held at Sharon's home church, the Staunton Street Apostolic Church, pastored by her father, Reverend Greene

Kitchen. Three very memorable things took place at that meeting. First, I was granted my credentials with the United Pentecostal Church International. Second, I got to see the workings of the organization as the Virginia District was organized in that conference. My uncle, Rev. Roy Hall, was their first superintendent, and Reverend McGloskey was their first secretary treasurer. And third, it would be my only time to be with the spiritual giant, Reverend A. T. Morgan. (He passed away at the following General Conference in Tulsa, Oklahoma.) After that spring conference, Sharon and I drove to Charleston to visit with one of our favorite people, Rev. Danny Scott, and I asked him to perform our marriage ceremony. We made that moment a reality on August 4, 1967.

Sharon has been often heard to say, "I married Edwin, and he was a God-called minister, and my lot in life has been to follow him wherever God's will leads." The initial test was the fact that I would attend Texas Bible College in Houston, Texas. The emotion-filled wedding seemed almost like a funeral to some, because they all knew that within the week we would be leaving for Texas.

Brother Scott asked, "Who gives this woman to be married to this man?"

Sharon's father answered, "Her mother and I." At that moment her six-year-old ring bearer, Davey, began to snub. Before long the whole wedding party had tears streaming down their faces, and the guests started to join in. Eventually all were able to regain their composure and Brother Scott proceeded.

Brother Scott said, "Edwin, repeat after me. I, Edwin, take thee, Sharon."

When I repeated it, my lack of intimidation let me boldly say, "I Edwin." The volume shocked my new bride. Remember that Sharon delivers messages with her elbow. She politely elbowed me in the ribs, so I repeated the rest of the vows much softer.

The preacher's wife thing was for real now. I had been holding revivals since before I had my driver's license. On our honeymoon, Sharon looked up the name and number of the local UPCI pastor and asked for directions to the church. Even though we had just been married on the preceding Friday night, it was engrained in her that you go to Sunday School where ever you are, no matter what is going on in your life. After church that morning the pastor recognized Sharon and met me, her new husband. Upon learning that I was a preacher, he insisted that I preach that evening. I did preach, and Sharon loves to tell that I did not sound like, an 18-year-old but "like a man that had been preaching for 20 years." She often would say, "I am his biggest fan." Her father and mother had molded into her character this loyalty to the ministry. By the first of September we were in Houston, Texas. On September 18, I enrolled as a student in Texas Bible College.

The trip to Houston was pretty much uneventful. The two-day, 1,200-mile trip was made in the second car, a 1960 Chevy Impala that I had built from a couple of wrecked vehicles. On the last leg of the trip I showed some signs of fatigue, so Sharon volunteered to drive for a little while. A little while turned into several hundred miles, and before we realized it we were in the hustle of the East-Tex Freeway, U.S. 59. This small town couple was suddenly in the midst of a city of 2.5 million people. On that crowded city freeway we couldn't find a place to stop and let me drive. The freeway dropped us downtown into the midst of an African-American part of town. This was the year before Martin Luther King Junior was assassinated. We stopped at a signal light. We were both pretty nervous.

I said, "I'll take it from here." Instead of letting her slide over me, with me sliding under to take the wheel, I did something foolish and dangerous. I jumped out of the right side, ran around to the left side of the car, and jerked the door open in traffic into the side of a rapidly moving pick-up truck. I was almost killed, but we were in Houston.

Sharon sat in the wrecked car and waited, panic

stricken. I went on foot for help. There was no other place to go besides an African-American nightclub and bar. I walked in to call the police and report the accident. It seemed to take forever for the police to arrive. Having arrived into Houston in the evening rush hour traffic, and having suffered a door torn from our car, with darkness setting in and with Latinos and African-Americans everywhere in sight, for this girl and boy from a town with only 6% of the population black, we might as well been in a foreign country doing a missions trip with David Livingston. Yet Sharon was a minister's wife, and she had said, "I'll follow him."

We finished the accident report, and I acquired some rope from the black man into whose vehicle I had opened my car door. I tied the door onto the car as well as I could.

The police officer said, "As for the safety of your car I have little to offer. The list of stolen cars in Houston takes a day to read." We pulled out the directions to the Bible college and motored off to 816 Evergreen Drive.

Now it was in the letter that there would be an apartment waiting on us. When we arrived at the college, not only was there not an apartment, but because we had arrived two weeks early (so we could get settled into our new life), there was no one at the college who really knew what was going on. Sharon always remembers there was no apartment. A man, who was the dean of the single men, allowed us to unload our wrecked car into an empty dorm room, and he gave us directions to the Holiday Inn on Wayside Drive, across the Gulf Freeway from the motel where Lee Harvey Oswald had stayed the night before he went to Dallas to kill President Kennedy.

When we got into the room, Sharon quickly closed the drapes and said, "I'm not sure that I am ready to face what's out there yet."

The next day, when we awoke from a dead-tired-night's rest, Sharon opened the windows to look out at the new world. Under the glory of morning sunlight her eternal optimism wicked up the steel of her life, which she did not know that she even possessed until that moment. She would draw upon it many times for the rest of her life.

Sharon looked at me and said, "Well, it's time to do it." After the usual morning routine of getting ready, we proceeded to the Patricia Manor Apartments where there was supposed to be an apartment reserved for us, yet, "there was no apartment." The management sent us a half a mile away to a sister complex, not as nice or as safe, on Telephone Road. There we were able to secure a furnished apartment.

We collected our belongings from the men's dorm and moved them to the apartment on Telephone Road. Our bed for the first night was only the blankets that we had brought from our household and wedding shower back in Huntington. The apartment complex already had guests/residents of the type that, back in West Virginia, would be entertained only by folks with unclean lifestyles. We did not yet know that even the nicest of homes in the Gulf Coast area have a daily battle with "roaches." We were horrified to learn that this new world had new battles—some big, some small—but everything in life can be handled by finding out from the veterans of life how to wage the war.

In our attempt to get acclimated to this new environment we visited the campus, wondering who was available for us to share our time and challenges with. A nice couple from Indiana, Kandus and Linda Rust (along with Carrie, their cute baby girl), were there doing the same thing. They were a few years older than us, and we gladly began a friendship based on helping each other solve the next problem.

Kandis and I found employment at the Pasadena School District, going to work on the campus of the 4000-student Pasadena High School.

Since Telephone Road was not the safest address to have, Sharon busied herself looking for another, safer address. She was able to find an available apartment near the junction of Wayside Drive and Lawndale. In those days Lawndale was considered a nicer place to live. We were only going to live at Lawndale for one month and then an apartment would become available for us on campus. The driveway there was a bit narrow, and the old '60 Chevy was a little wider than Sharon's mother's Rambler. You guessed it. After a few trips in and out of the driveway (in making the turns to get into the carport), Sharon managed to do to the right side of the car something similar to what the initial accident had done to the left side. (She now has a little list: two rear fenders of a Volkswagen, the side of a Pontiac, and perhaps a half a dozen tires and rims in potholes over the years. But it's as she says, "One incident every few years isn't too bad. Nobody has gotten hurt.")

Life on the campus was much more enjoyable. She interacted with all of the T.B.C. wives' functions. Participating in a model for ladies ministry reminded her of the large ladies group her mother led at home. She had no problem adapting and learning the customs as well as the cuisine of the south-Texas world. She made it a point that even though the apartment where we were living may not have been up to date, she was determined to decorate and remodel it to make a comfortable place for her husband to retreat to after his hectic week of study and work. Her tasks accomplished for me were: pay our tithes, budget the grocery list, pack my lunch, have me a meal ready when I get home, pay the rent, put gas in the car, and even buy a new '68 Volkswagen Bug. Sharon was quite the steward when you realize I was only making $49.75 a week. She saved a dime a day by walking to Hanel's Grocery, where she would sometimes buy a cola to sip on. She would make that cola last as long as she could while working in the apartment or visiting with friends.

Chapter 7
Fledgling Wings

Because of the revival services that we were able to preach between semesters, we were able to pay off our '68 Volkswagen, and with the help of Brother Kitchen, we eventually traded it in on a new 1970 Pontiac.

You might be aware that Houston, Texas, was a utopia of Pentecostal churches in 1967. Some of the greatest pastors that were available anywhere in the world ministered in Houston. With this populace of churches around us, there was a constant stream of outstanding guest preachers and speakers visiting the campus for chapel services. My late father-in-law was one of those men.

I got to meet Rev. A. D. Urshan and hear him minister in the last month of his life. He took a large group of us to "Kip's," a "Big Boy" restaurant on Griggs Road in Houston, for a lunch one day. About 15 to 20 of us joined him. Before we ate, he led us into a prayer that was beyond the norm.

In his Persian accent he said, "Let us all stand together. The world acts the way it chooses to act all the time. We are children of God, and we should always be ready to exhibit the love we have for Jesus. Pray and talk in tongues, like you would if you were in church. Let the Holy Ghost touch everyone in this place." And we did. Following the prayer he taught us the "Urshan Family Meal Time Song."

At one time or another, the best Gospel preachers of the United Pentecostal Church came through those doors to minister to us. In such a service, Brother C. L. Dees brought West Virginia's Willie Johnson to minister. As you might imagine, if you have ever been in a Bible college chapel service, at the conclusion of her ministry a great conviction and burden to pray swept the student body. We fell to our knees around the altar, and Sister Johnson began to move through the praying young ministers, laying her hands on us and praying over us. I know she didn't know it was me. She did not know me that well, and furthermore, my face was down to the carpet in sobbing prayer (the way I had seen my Father pray). Without warning, she laid both hands on my head and prophesied in my ear. I had heard it before.

"The Lord has called you," she said. "Today, I come to tell you that you are a chosen vessel. Think not what you shall say in the hours that you are called upon. I have touched your mind and your heart so that your mouth will be filled with my words. You shall stand before great men of this world and declare the truth of the Lord Jesus Christ. Fear not, for I am with you, saith the LORD. Thousands of thousands will believe at the witness that you give of the LORD. You shall see the world and be instrumental in the spreading of this *message* of *truth*. You must remain humble because none of your future is of your doing. I AM the Lord, and I send you forth into the harvest. Remember always that your steps are ordered of the LORD. Be thou faithful and faint not, for to whom much is given, much is required. I am with you to-day, and I will be with you when you feel you are least able to fulfill this *call* and *command*." This was the second time she spoke into my life, but it would not be the last time I would encounter her insight into my life.

It would have been so easy to attend a big church like she had grown up in, but without any reluctance Sharon agreed to attend a small home-mission church. Because my parents were pastoring a home-mission church back in Nitro, West Virginia, I felt it important to help the same effort while in school. Without complaint, every weekend she went with me. We attended twice on Sundays. She taught a Sunday School class. She helped with the music and singing, as well as enthusiastically supporting me anytime that I was the speaker.

As the annual youth week approached on the United Pentecostal Church's calendar, the young preacher couples on the campus were abuzz contemplating as to whether or not they would be called on by some kind pastor to be the evangelist during their youth week revival. Because I was a freshman, I was at the bottom of the pecking order in recognition for availability to be a guest preacher. Almost all of the upperclassmen were assigned to preaching appointments. Sharon was an immense comfort to my ego, as I was somewhat used to the "favored son" status back home.

She said, "Why don't you just pray and see what God really wants?" While I was praying back in the prayer closet, there was a knock at the apartment door. Sharon answered the door to find Brother Brian Chellette, one of the professors at the college.

Brother Chellette asked if I was at home or had I gone to work yet. She asked him to wait, and she brought me to the door. He explained that there was a pastor on the west side of town, Brother Lambert, who had just called. Brother Chellette had remembered from an earlier conversation that we were well known as a young ministering couple before we came to Houston. The next three years would prove invaluable to us, because we would be blessed beyond measure by Pastor and Mrs. Charles E. Lambert, their family, and the Gospel Truth Pentecostal Church at 5102 Center Street.

When we arrived at the Gospel Truth Pentecostal Church that first night, we were taken by the genuine love of God that was demonstrated at the church. The uniqueness of the pastor's wife, Molly Lambert, put her in a class all by herself. From this cherub-faced, older lady Sharon learned some of the richest lessons about being a pastor's wife.

"Sharon," she said, "You can't please them, so don't even try. If you make it a point to go around and shake everybody's hand they will think that you're trying to show off your hat, shoes, dress or hairdo. If you don't try to visit with everyone they will accuse you of being stuck-up. So just be yourself, and don't take yourself too seriously. Love God, and be faithful to attend church. Support your husband, and make sure you are ready for the rapture. If you get that done, you'll be a great pastor's wife."

During the three and one-half years that we attended, ministered and helped at Gospel Truth, Sharon taught Sunday School, was the church musician, worked in the dinners and bazaars of the church, and actively spent her Saturdays walking the streets of west Houston—helping me to build up bus routes that brought scores of children of all ethnicities to the church.

A lover of children, Sharon was often heard to say, "I could take them all home with me."

Our first year home on summer vacation, I met the district board a second time, during camp meeting, and I was approved for the next step in ministerial credentials, a General License. Although I was formally an assistant to the pastor of the second-oldest UPCI church in Houston, one of the presbyters serving on the district board argued that I should wait until I was out of college and pastoring fulltime before being approved for the advancement. Brother D. W. Durst, the man who baptized my Dad, was quick to point out that the very presbyter who was challenging my approval was bi-vocational himself and not yet fulltime after 35 years.

Brother Durst declared, "I think Brother Harper is already time and a half."

We returned to school, and in watching the lives of the ministers in Houston, we developed a deeper personal commitment to God. Building on the great foundation that our parents had already laid in our lives, we became multi-dimensional, adding the influences of the Kilgores, Williams, Fausses, Guidrozes, Dees, and of course the Lamberts. At the end of the schooling at Texas Bible College we would say,

"Edwin got a Th.B., but Sharon got a P.H.T. (Put Husband Through)." Sharon has helped to "Put Her Husband Through" every challenge ever since.

As the time had passed in Houston, we were able to move to nicer addresses. Our sixth move allowed us to spend the last two years living just two blocks away from the home of Reverend and Mrs. C. L. Dees. As nice as it was, still crime was everywhere in Houston. Sharon spent the last year supplementing our income by working as an inventory auditor at J. C. Penny's at the Northwest Mall. Sharon had come home on a breezy, pretty, spring day, and she decided to let some fresh air into the apartment while she lay across the bed to rest. About 45 minutes later I arrived from the church. As I pulled into the complex on T. C. Jester, I saw a helicopter hovering over the bayou and a police S.W.A.T. team swarming the area. I ran to the apartment and found the door open.

Frightened, I rushed into the room and said, "What are you doing laying in here with the door open?"

"Well, I am resting," said Sharon. "What's wrong with that?"

"Oh, nothing, except there are police everywhere outside. There is something bad happening."

Later we were informed that a burglary had occurred four blocks away and the suspects were hiding in the bayou culverts just outside our apartment. It was the "Wild West" there in Texas, but all was well for us.

During my senior year of college, we visited the nearby Greater Bethel Pentecostal Church, pastored by Oliver and Orland Ray Fauss. During service there, Sister Willie Johnson approached me and prophesied over me, repeating again verbatim the same words she had spoken over me on those earlier occasions. Also while visiting there, the Fausses strongly encouraged us to stay in Houston at the church where we were assisting (Gospel Truth Pentecostal Church) because that church's pastor, his family, and the church board really wanted us to remain and become the pastor of the church. However, we had sought God, and we agreed together that God's will for us was not in Houston, Texas. The salary would have been great. The car allowance would have been grand, and the thought of a new home was fabulous. Sharon, though, was more moved by the tug of the Holy Ghost than the idea of a new home. She had married a "man of God," and she felt compelled to follow me.

Earlier in the year we had been invited to Dupo, Illinois, to preach another youth week revival at the church pastored by the soon-outgoing missionary, James Wood. The revival had been so successful that the church contacted us, shortly after we left Houston, to ask us if we would consider allowing our name to stand as a candidate to become their next pastor. We prayerfully responded with a yes.

In the meantime, we traveled home to West Virginia in time to attend the East Central District Conference, which was held in Morgantown, West Virginia, at the Riverside Apostolic Church, pastored by Reverend Hayward Saffle. At that conference, I met the district board and was approved for Ordination. The great privilege of being ordained was magnified by the fact that the Minister of Ordination for our conference that year was Reverend J. T. Pugh, the General Home Missions Director of the United Pentecostal Church International. We knelt side by side and felt the enduing warmth and flow of the Holy Ghost anointing engulf us as Brother Pugh laid his hands on us along with the district board; Superintendent E. C. Sowards, District Secretary Greene Kitchen, Presbyters Hayward Saffle, Ralph McIntyre, J. C. Cole, D. W. Durst and Brother Roy Riffle.

At that conference, the pastors of the district were very kind to begin booking and scheduling revivals with us. As kind as they were, Sharon was not anxious to begin a life as a traveling evangelist. Every summer during our time in Bible college, we had traveled and preached across West Virginia, Maryland, Kentucky and Ohio. We had slept in attics, unfinished bedrooms, and one-room cabins with an outhouse and a path. Sharon had shared with me that the Lord had given her a message that her life would be spent as a helpmeet to the ministry of the *pastor.*

During that conference, a call came to the Riverside Church office from the First Pentecostal Faith Tabernacle, 620 Minnie Avenue (Minnie was also Sharon's mother's first name), Dupo, Illinois, with the message that we had been elected as the pastors of the church, and that we were expected in Dupo within the month. It was with some joy that Sharon was able to go from pastor's wife to pastor's wife and thank them, yet at the same time tell them that she was sorry, but that she and I would not be able to be their guest for the time of revival. As we were leaving the conference, I commented to Sharon's father that the people at Riverside sure were wonderful, and it sure would be great if that church could move its address to a nicer location. Brother Kitchen laid his hand on my shoulder and said, "Brother Harper, you're the man to get that job done." Only time would tell that Greene Kitchen was indeed a prophet.

Chapter 8
The Quiver of Joash

Our time in Dupo, Illinois, served as our A. I. T. (Advanced Individual Training). Before we left West Virginia, we did preach one revival for our longtime favorite, Reverend D. W. and Sister Pearl Durst, in Charleston. After that revival, we moved to Illinois. My parents had given us a graduation present in cash. It was enough to buy new furniture for the parsonage in Dupo.

Brother Kitchen gave us some very good financial advice, "Buy the furniture with the money, but set up a savings account for yourselves, and make a furniture payment back in to that account just as if you had bought the furniture through a finance company. In three years you'll have your money back, plus the interest you would have paid the finance company, plus the interest your money will draw in savings. If you need new furniture later, you will be able to borrow the money from yourself."

As the new pastorate began, it was clear that Sharon was very gifted with her social skills. Working among the ladies of the church, she moved them as a leader in prayer and matters of the Ladies Auxiliary efforts. (That was what it was called before the term Ladies Ministry.) They worked together and raised enough money to install central air-conditioning in the sanctuary. The young people gravitated to her as well as the older saints. The church began to grow.

During the first year at the church we were able to obtain health insurance through the UPCI. This simply meant that we could make plans on starting a family. We did, and on June 23, 1972, in the county seat of St. Clair County, in the city of Belleville, the beautiful, olive-skinned Brigitte Danielle came into our world. Although it is perhaps not one of the old songs of the faith, on that day when Sharon held her beautiful little girl she started singing, "I'm the happiest girl in the whole USA, zippa-de-do-dah, thank you, Lord." It was such a joy. Having such fond affections for the Bectons, then General Secretary of the UPCI, we invited Brother Becton to be a guest at the church for the dedication of our new baby girl. Since it was summer and camp meeting time, it was an exciting opportunity to take Danielle to the West Virginia/ East Central District Camp and see our family and friends. When we entered the tabernacle, there was Reverend D. W. Durst, an icon in both of our lives. Sharon made it a point to take Danielle to that old prophet and let him hold the baby and pray for her.

Historically, the Dupo congregation had been hard on pastors and especially hard on pastor's wives. After one year, the attitude from several church members toward us did not allow the church history to have any kind exception from the rule.

Sharon was busy in the kitchen of the parsonage, which was a three-bedroom apartment built over the Sunday School classrooms of a basement area that was originally meant to be the basement of the whole church complex. (When a previous pastor had needed a place to live the church body had decided to put a parsonage apartment where the foyer and restrooms of the main sanctuary would have been. The church had done well under the ministry of Rev. E. J. McClintock and a metal and masonry sanctuary was built and attached to the original build.) I came into the apartment from the church and announced that I had just encountered an angel (the same voice that I had an experience with in Nitro when I was 16 years old) in the sanctuary during my private Morning Prayer session. I told her how the angel had handed me a quiver of arrows and had told me to take the "quiver of Joash" and smite the ground. I described my fear and was reminded of the scripture, so I beat the floor continually until the angel had said "enough." I shared that the angel had informed me that it was going to be a year of battle but that the enemy of the souls of Dupo was going to be defeated through the conflict. I had no sooner finished telling her about the amazing encounter when there came a knock at the front door of the parsonage. When Sharon answered the door, there stood the husband of the woman that had assisted Sharon through her pregnancy and delivery of Danielle. In fact, this was a man that I had personally won to the Lord. The member at the door was the son-in-law of a retired preacher that had been involved in every church problem that had gone on in the church for many years.

The man at the door—a former agnostic, the head of the math department at a respected university, and a person who basically, genuinely loved the church—asked the question, "Is pastor available? I need to talk to him." We invited him in, and a discussion followed that informed me that I was taking too much authority as pastor. As always, the first question was, "Can we see the church books?"

I had followed the advice of my wise father-in-law: Since we had been at the church for only a year, I had not changed anything about the operation of the church from what it was when we came. Thus, it was an odd request for the pastor to show a member the books, since the church still had the same treasurer and the same money policies in place that had existed for the past 15 years. The problem was that repairs had been done: all the broken windows that had been missing for the first six months were repaired by the me, at my own expense; the bathrooms had been cleaned and painted by me, the pastor, at my expense; the basement had been cleaned and repairs made to make the Sunday school rooms more presentable—so it seemed obvious that money was being taken out of the treasury without proper business meeting approval. Of course that was preposterous, because the real reason was there were enough new people coming to the church that if something wasn't done quickly then the old, controlling faction was about to lose its death grip on the church.

When it was explained that the church treasurer had the books and that they were welcome to give her a call, the money issue was immediately off the table. A new list was developed. The pastor spent too much time with other ministers. We traveled to West Virginia too often. Not everyone had access to the pastor. We need more anointing in our services. The other ministers that were natives of the local church needed to be invited to come home and speak more often. Yet the biggie was, "We're afraid that you are going to let these younger and newer converts have too much say in the administration of the church."

The phone calling began, and one Sunday morning a dear lady stopped Sharon in the hallway and said, "I've got a goodly group of people together and we are on your side."

The lifetime of training with her father and mother came alive, and Sharon responded, "We don't have a side. Brother Harper is everyone's pastor, and we want the church to have peace and harmony so that this revival can continue."

As relentless as church problems can be, Sharon kept assuring me that God would give me the right directives at the right time. One morning she reminded me that it might be good to seek out an unbiased older minister and just talk with him. After prayer that morning, I took a drive over to Gateway College of Evangelism and spent the day visiting with Reverend Raymond Kloeper, the president of the college. By the end of the day, with a rich story from his past, I had obtained a reference point as to what I might be able to use as guidance. Two days went by, and I came up from the Morning Prayer and shared with Sharon the story that he had related to me.

I then told my wife, "Instead of engaging in the public drama that Brother Kloeper had used in the church in Mississippi by calling the people at the core of the problem to the front of the church and publicly giving them letters of transfer to another church, I am going to go to their homes and give them these letters without involving the whole church."

Sharon remembered a similar time in her father's life and said, "It would be best if you took some of the elders of the church with you."

I called four good men and asked them to take a car ride with me. Once I had picked them up and we were on our way to the first home, I told the brethren, "Tonight I am not asking you to agree with me or disagree. I simply want you to be witnesses to what I say and do."

We pulled up to the first house, got out, knocked on the door, and waited. The man that had first come to the parsonage (the day of my encounter with the angel) answered the door, and he showed total shock. He nervously invited us in. Although I had expected to make two stops that evening, we quickly realized that our travel time had been shortened, because both of the couples that we were going to visit that night were there together. What was surprising to the men with me was the paper that the two couples were working on, which was lying on the table. They were busy crafting a petition for our removal as pastor of the church.

I made no reference to the paper, but in the presence of the men I pulled two envelopes out of my pocket, handed one to each man, and said, "Since that you are so unhappy with the ministry and church here, rather than being a part of something foolish and hurting your family and perhaps damning their soul, it will be best for you to find a place of worship and a pastor that suits your taste, rather than promoting this confusion here at this church. Take this letter that does not tarnish your name and go start over afresh."

At that point the second man, who had been a chronic backslider, and with whom I had worked to get him back in church, jumped up and said, "You can't do this."

I softly responded, "I just did, and you need to accept it. If you don't, I will be forced to take steps to dis-fellowship you from the United Pentecostal Church."

Both couples lashed out.

One of the older men said, "I did not know why we were coming here, but I am sorry, and yet glad at the same time, that I got to see this. For the sake of all of us you need to do exactly what the pastor has said."

I interrupted and said, "I am going to pray. Dear Lord Jesus, here are two families that you love more than words can express. I don't think that I can pastor them, but you know in this area where there is a ministry that can help them and their families to make Heaven." At this point I was weeping, and the men that were with me were weeping. Eventually the two couples began to weep. I continued, "I pray today that we all realize that this is not about personality or power, but this is about all of us being able to have peace in our souls. Bless these families and guide them in a new direction and let us look back on this day and say it was good for our salvation; in the name of Jesus Christ. Amen."

When I got back to the parsonage Sharon was still on her knees in the bedroom praying. She came out with the baby in her arms and said, "God is taking care of everything. I don't know how, but come Sunday, things will be better."

(Years later at a General Conference in St. Louis, Missouri, both couples would seek us out on separate occasions and thank us for the stand that I took saying that I had saved their lives. Both men ended up being ordained ministers in the UPCI.)

Sunday morning came, and it was a good day. Because I had taken a stand, a total of seventeen people were not present—because they were the old faction that had notoriously fired the pastors in the past. The two young couples that had received their transfer letters had been coached by the older retired preacher father-in-law who was historically the trouble leader. The seventeen scattered to three different churches. This element spread the news that they were leaving the church. When the community heard that they were gone, people who had stayed away from the church for years showed up on Sunday morning. It was a good day. For months we had wanted to have over 100 in attendance yet had only reached 92. With the removal of the 17 dissenters, 107 people were in attendance at Sunday School.

On the heels of this painful year, a revival broke out in the church. In the course of the next two years, 257 people received the Holy Ghost. The choir that Sharon developed grew, as well as the Sunday morning and Sunday night attendance.

Sharon was out walking one day, pushing her baby in the stroller. Down the street from the church, she recognized a small three-bedroom house hidden in the weeds. The weeds had grown up so tall that you had to be looking for the house to find it. Proverbs 31 says that a "...virtuous woman...findeth a field... [for her husband] and buyeth it." The fact is that every piece of land that we have lived on in our married life was a property she had identified and chosen. We bought the house and lot for $6000.00. I remodeled it, and Sharon decorated it. (When we eventually moved away from Dupo we were able to sell the house for $14,700.00.) This home allowed us to turn the parsonage area into Sunday School rooms and give the attendance a chance to grow. The growth and revival was significant enough that an addition was necessary to extend the back of the sanctuary. A nice colonial porch and entrance were added. A choir loft and baptistery were added in the new addition and the previously flat ceiling was raised and changed to a lofty, cathedral style.

Chapter 9
Faith Without Fear

I fit right in to the country culture of the Dupo area. A great friendship was formed with Reverend Terry Russell, who had grown up in the Dupo Church. At that time he was pastoring in Connellsville, Illinois. Sharon knew that we two liked to fish. Being that was years before mobile phones, she became worried one evening because we were later than usual in returning from the farm lake where we fished, down at Red Bud. She and Judy, Terry's wife, were waiting on us when we got home. It was a great relief, but also a shocking surprise. We pulled three washtubs of crappie out of the trunk and back seat of the car. Sharon said, "Well, if you will clean them it looks like we are going to have a fish dinner to raise money for the new addition you are putting on the church." The end result was almost a thousand dollars raised in the process.

When the church you are pastoring has revival, you don't pick and choose who comes to God or how. You just serve. One of the new families that started coming to the church was a young couple, both from homes of Pentecostal pastors in cities distant from Dupo. As happens in many young couples' lives, they had their financial difficulties. Unfortunately the husband turned to the wrong source to help with their financial struggle. He borrowed money from a loan shark. One day he came to me crying, and he said the lender had told him that if he didn't have the money by such-and-such date they were going to kill him. He told me the date and time when they were coming to collect. I told him I would see what I could do. After praying I was inspired to go to the bank and borrow that amount of money and be at his home when the collector arrived. It was a warm fall evening. I drove to his mobile home, and in the dark I sat down on the tongue of the trailer. Sure enough, at the time he said they were coming, a set of headlights lit up the driveway. I waited to see what was happening. Two men got out of the van. They stopped at the end of the sidewalk and began shouting the name of the husband, demanding that he come out of the home. I sat on the front end of the trailer until I heard the storm door open. I got up, walked into the light of the porch lamp, shocked because I knew the two men.

They said, "Reverend, what in the #@&% are you doing here?"

"Oh, I thought I might try to keep some folks from going to hell tonight," I replied.

"This ain't none of your business. You get in your car and get out of here."

"Why are you guys here?" I asked.

"Because this fat jerk owes money, and we're here to make sure he pays it or doesn't cheat anybody else."

I turned to the husband, who was trembling on the porch, and I asked him how much he owed them. He responded, and I walked out to the two men and told them I had come to pay the debt and keep all of them out of trouble. The younger man, the son of the other, choked up and said, "I can't believe this."

I called him by name and told him, "This is exactly what Jesus did for all of us at Calvary."

His choke turned into a sob, and his dad let out a curse and began wiping the tears from his own face. To make a long story short, all three of them and their families have attended the General Conference of the UPCI. All are born again, and the older gentleman was right with God when he died. By the way, they gave the money back to me about two months later, after they had been filled with the Holy Ghost.

There was a Dupo policeman living in the next block north of the church. He stopped by the parsonage one evening and asked me if I would go with him because they had a bad situation in a motel across town. A man was holding another man at gunpoint and threatening to kill him over a woman and was promising that then he was going to take his own life. He was asking for a minister. When I arrived on the scene, Bob told the man that he had a preacher.

The man shouted out, "I want to hear him talk." When I told him who I was, he responded that just last month he had come to a Sunday evening service and had heard me preach. After a couple of courteous exchanges, I told him that I needed to come inside the motel room to talk to him. I walked in without his answer.

There he stood, holding a large-caliber revolver up to the side of this man's head. I called him by name and walked over to their sides. The man in the chair was trembling, and with a quivering voice he told me that he didn't want to die. The man with the gun reassured me that he was going to blow the man's brains out and then kill himself.

I calmly said, "Well, if you're going to die, let me pray for you both before it's over." I asked for God's mercy and told the Lord to be kind when He dealt with their wretched souls, and that I didn't want to see them go to hell. I never closed my eyes. I literally was watching and praying—with good cause. In a moment with both of them weeping, I reached out and took hold of the barrel of the gun, and I slowly pushed it to point toward the floor. I kept on praying in the Holy Ghost, and he released his hold on the pistol. When we walked out of the motel, the policeman, Bob, commented that I was either the craziest man that he knew or the bravest. I never again heard from the would-be victim. The man with the gun did come and get baptized. I never heard from either again, but God gave me favor.

Sharon worked so hard, walking the streets and knocking on doors, building a bus route for the Sunday School and then teaching her class every Sunday. Together, we knocked every door in Dupo, Cahokia, Columbia and East Carondelet.

The first service in the newly remodeled sanctuary was on Easter Sunday. The service started with a choir song and a baptismal service. I had worked all night finishing up some final things. At 6:30 AM I came home to rest for a while. Sharon lay Danielle in the bed with me and went to the church to dust all of the pews and arrange the choir loft so everything would look nice for the Easter crowd. The crowds came that year and the next. On Easter Sunday of the next year, 1974, a record was set with 373 in attendance.

At the end of that year I came in from another

prayer meeting, and said, "Sharon, I have dreamed the same dream three times. We are leaving here and going to a city with a round building that looks like a crown. In the dream I baptize a tall, black-headed man wearing black glasses, in a baptistery that is down in the floor."

"When are we going to do this?" she asked.

"Before the end of the year. God will tell us when the time is right."

Chapter 10
Winds of Change

On the second Sunday in December there was an event and an enlightening conversation with Sharon that allowed me to know that it was time to tell the church we were leaving. That night after I preached, I announced that Reverend Daniel Seagraves would be the guest preacher next Sunday. Then I read a kind letter in which I resigned the church, effective December 30, 1974. For a church that had been known to run preachers off, a real phenomenon happened. Without exception, every person came by and asked us to reconsider and stay. (By the way, the church went on to elect Reverend Seagraves as their pastor, and he eventually served the church for seven years.)

Sharon's father had raised money to buy buses to begin a bus ministry at her home church in Huntington, West Virginia. In those days, Reverend Roy Gerald of Lemay Ferry, South St. Louis, sold used school buses. Sharon's father bought two buses from him. The men of Huntington came out to drive the buses home in the fourth week of December. We loaded up the buses with as much of our belongings as we could and let them haul those things back to West Virginia for us.

The morning of December 31, 1974, Sharon, Danielle and I pulled away from our little house at 628 Minnie Avenue in Dupo, Illinois. Several of the church members came out to see us off. We locked up our little house, said farewell to the huge crowd of well wishers, and got in the car. As the car pulled away, all those members, young and old, stood in the middle of the street waving and wiping tears from their eyes. We drove home to Sharon's parents' home in Huntington, West Virginia. That night I preached at the annual "Watch Night Service" at the Staunton Street Apostolic Church. On New Year's Day, we all rose late because we had been up into the wee hours of the morning. Sharon's mother prepared her normal breakfast feast for the family who had gathered at the home for the occasion. Breakfast was over at about 1:30 pm, and there came a phone call.

At that time, Sharon's father was the West Virginia District Superintendent. Reverend Hayward Saffle was the pastor of the Riverside Apostolic Church in Morgantown and the presbyter of that section. His phone call began with a statement informing Superintendent Kitchen that, as of last evening, he had surprised his congregation and announced his resignation and retirement as their pastor. When asked what his plans were, he immediately said that, other than informing of his decision, he also wanted the phone number of "Brother Harper" in Illinois.

Sharon's father said, "Brother Saffle, your timing of this call is incredible. Brother Harper is sitting here with me right now. He just resigned the church in Illinois and his last day there was December 30. He preached for us last night, and he is going to be preaching a New Year's revival for us starting tomorrow evening. Would you like to speak to him now?"

With that, the phone was handed to me, and the discussion that followed set a date in two weeks for Sharon, Danielle and me to visit the Morgantown church and be examined by the congregation and church elders. The Pentecostal colloquial term is "Try Out."

The revival services at "Staunton Street" were very successful. There are people that received the Holy Ghost in that meeting that, as late as the writing of this book, are still members of the Huntington church. Some are in the ministry, pastoring.

After the second Saturday night meeting, Sharon and I headed out for Morgantown so we could be in Sunday morning service at the Riverside Apostolic

Church. In those days, the interstate system in West Virginia was not yet complete, so the trip was intermittent between the two-lane, curvy, mountain roads and an occasional straight stretch of four lanes. Once we turned north on I-79 out of Clarksburg, West Virginia, we saw a mileage sign: "Morgantown 26 miles." As we counted off the miles, suddenly we popped up over the horizon just before the Westover exit (#152). There on the hilltop in the distance, all lit up at two o'clock in the morning, was the West Virginia University Coliseum. It is round and looks like a crown with its accent lights shining on it.

I said, "Sharon, that is the building I told you about in my dream." Four years prior, the interstate had not yet been built entering Morgantown, and we had not ventured to that side of the city during the 1971 District Conference when we were ordained. As we gazed at that crown-like building, just as it was foreseen in my dream, it was truly a road sign in our spiritual journey.

That Sunday morning, as we walked into the foyer of the church located at 110 Monongahela Boulevard, I commented to Sharon, "The last thing I ever had said to me as we were leaving after the District Conference in 1971, was said to me by your Dad."

"What was that?"

"Well, I had said that these people deserved to be

in a better location and have a nicer facility. Your father laid his hand on my shoulder and said, 'Brother Harper, you're the man to get that job done.' Sharon, I truly believe that this is the will of God for our lives."

Even with the strong implications in every direction that made me feel so positive about the possibility of coming to Morgantown, in my talks with God I put a fleece before the Lord: "If it is Your perfect will for us to come to this city, I ask that You speak directly to Sharon and have her tell me that she has heard Your voice." Early on in our marriage I had learned that Sharon was a praying woman. It was not uncommon for me to go to bed at night with Sharon weeping and praying down in the floor. Sometimes when I would get out of bed the next morning, I would find that she had prayed all night. I knew that God could speak to her.

The Sunday morning and evening services defined the matching spirits and desires of the church and Sharon and I. Sharon played her accordion and sang with an endearing anointing, and I preached as well or better than I ever had. The history of Sharon with the youth of the district resulted in campground buddies gathered around her, and the men identified with my downhome demeanor. There was, however, an interesting introduction for Sharon as she was being shown through the Sunday School classes while I was teaching. After seeing the classes, Brother Norwood took her to the Sunday School office to introduce her to the office staff. There she was greeted by the Sunday School secretary, who was dressed in a mini-skirt, with short-cut hair and make-up. When telling me about the encounter she remarked, "Looks like it might take a little more work than we had at Dupo."

Ruth and Roscoe Dawson entertained us at dinner, and then they chauffeured us back and forth to the Hotel Morgan. The Dawsons had been like fixtures at the West Virginia Campground where he had worked as a maintenance man and Ruth had been our choir director at youth camp. Roscoe was one of the church's elders, along with Norwood Dulin, and Jack Dawson (no relation to Roscoe).

The church was looking for a Bible teacher as well as a pastor and preacher. Things had gone so well on Sunday that the elders of the church asked us to stay over and teach in the Tuesday evening prayer meeting and Bible study. The elders and I had a meeting on Monday evening, and Sharon had a good prayer meeting at the hotel. The meeting left me with a positive feeling. The men and I agreed that the church should hear at least four voices, so that when the church had come to a conclusion as to who would be their pastor, then the church members, elders, and the minister would not be in a second-guessing posture should difficulties develop in the future. It was also agreed that a new minister would not be formally elected as pastor until having been there for six months. At the end of the allotted time period, they would invite the United Pentecostal Church Superintendent of West Virginia to come and conduct an official election. If election showed that everyone was still pleased, then there would be a service to install Sharon and I as Pastor and Wife.

From Morgantown we traveled to Charleston to meet a request for a revival meeting at First Pentecostal Church with Reverend D. W. Durst, a longtime family friend. In fact, D. W. had wanted Sharon to be "his" daughter-in-law and was the man that had baptized my father (at the time a Church of God minister) in the name of the Lord Jesus Christ. When the Charleston meeting concluded, we went on to preach at Saint Albans for Reverend Maurice Stringer, the man who had baptized me. During the meeting at Saint Albans, we stayed with Sharon's parents in Huntington.

One morning I had risen early and had spent several hours talking with Sharon's father about the opportunity at hand. Later Sharon came out of the bedroom, eyes were red as though she had been crying.

Sharon said, "Edwin, I really need to talk to you." Immediately I followed her as she turned and went back into the bedroom. "Listen," she began, "I don't want you to think that I am crazy, but I just had a frightening thing to happen to me. I have been praying all morning about Morgantown. When I settled down from a spirit of travail and was quietly sitting in the floor, someone walked up behind me and said, 'Sharon, you and Edwin are going to Morgantown. You are not going because of talent or because he is a good preacher. You are going because this is My will for you. Do not fear. I will be with you.' Edwin what in the world just happened?"

I told her, "The first day that we were in Morgantown, so many things had happened pointing in that direction that I felt it was the will of God for our lives. In prayer I put a fleece out before the Lord and said that if it is Your perfect will for us to come to this city, I ask that You speak directly to Sharon and have her tell me that she has heard Your voice. Sharon, the fleece has been fulfilled. This is the perfect will of God for our lives." That evening Brother Jack Dawson called and said that the church had elected us as their new (six-month interim) pastors.

It was time to move. The church wanted us there the next Sunday, February 9, 1975. The first service at Riverside was filled with expectation. Since it was the Sunday before Valentine's Day, the Sunday School children did a special presentation. As was the standing custom of Sunday School superintendent Norwood Dulin, the children's choir was introduced as the "Biggest Little Choir East of the Mississippi." The program concluded with the singing of the song "Let Me Call You Sweetheart" by Elaine Joswick and her cousin Bill Dulin. At the end of the program a dozen red roses were given to Sharon, as she and I were welcomed as the new pastors of the church.

For the next week the Hotel Morgan was our home until we were able to rent a two-bedroom house with a basement at 44 Washington Street, Westover, West Virginia. We let Danielle stay in Huntington with Mama and Papa Kitchen while we traveled to Dupo, rented a U-Haul truck, and, with the help of some of the good people of the Dupo church, loaded up our furniture and headed for Morgantown, West Virginia. The men of the Riverside Church were waiting on us when we arrived. In a short time the truck was unloaded, beds were set up, and we were ready to "live."

As soon as the house was organized and we were reasonably settled in, a phone call came. The caller wanted to know if we would like some company. Being the gregarious person that Sharon is, she said, "Sure, come on over." What she didn't know was that the whole church was coming! They had organized an old fashioned "pounding"—the custom in which every member of the congregation would bring a pound of some food item to stock the pantry of the pastor's home. The Davisson and Shisler families had butchered a beef. To accommodate the meat, some other members had donated money to buy a freezer for our little family. The surprise was absolutely overwhelming.

Chapter 11
Divine Destiny

As you would expect, since Sharon and I had been trained by such a man as Reverend Greene Kitchen, who was so successful in building up a Sunday School, we certainly wanted to duplicate his success. Easter was then one month away. In Huntington, the church had conducted an annual Easter Attendance Campaign with the use of the colors gold and silver for competing teams. Sharon called her father and got the details on what and how to conduct the program. Because we were in the "University City" it was only natural that the colors for the Riverside Apostolic Church's Easter Attendance Campaign should be gold and blue, WVU's school colors and thus the state's colors. Capturing the wave of the excitement of a new pastor and a new start, everyone wanted to go to work to get people to church on Sunday mornings.

The church had not had anyone to receive the baptism of the Holy Ghost in over two years. There was only one man that was coming to the altar and seeking for the Spirit. Charles Lemley was a survivor of the "Battle of the Bulge" in World War II. He and his wife Mary were custodians at the Engineering Building on the Evansdale Campus of West Virginia University.

Sharon said to me, "We are going to have to pray Brother Lemley through so we can get on with revival." She made up her mind that it was going to happen sooner rather than later. At a Tuesday night Bible study, I closed my teaching by saying that Sister Harper and I believed that this was as good a night as any for Brother Lemley to receive the Holy Ghost. Forty minutes later, with Sister Harper on one side of Charles and me on the other, Charles Lemley began to speak in other tongues as the Spirit gave the utterance.

The logjam was broken and the spirit of revival was loose as the Lord began to demonstrate what can happen when people move with His Spirit in His perfect will. By the third Sunday of the campaign, 307 people were in the morning service. It was Friend Day, and it seemed that everyone wanted to share their fresh blessing with all of their friends. Easter was upon us and all were in hopes of an attendance that would break the old mark of 452, which was the record for 14 years. It was an incredible Easter, as the sanctuary filled and the classrooms in the basement ran out of room. When Norwood

Dulin came to the pulpit at the end of the service he could hardly contain himself. Sharon sat with her hands to her mouth as he read the new attendance record for the church: 519 people.

With tears streaming down her face Sharon said, "I thought my heart was going to jump out of my chest."

The reader must be reminded that church growth, in spite of its joys, also has challenges. Things had happened so fast in growth that the real identity of the congregation had not surfaced yet. The church had a Conqueror's Club, consisting of the young people ages 12-36, which had gone without oversight for several years, because the previous leadership figured that with them involved in something and raising a little money, they were out of his hair.

One Sunday evening, one of the youth members burst into my small office and shouted, "They're about to get into a fight downstairs." I was surprised because I was not aware that there was a meeting to be held.

I responded by getting up and going into the sanctuary and simply whispering into Sharon's ear, "The young people need you to help them downstairs." Unaware of what she would face, she went into a classroom where the young married couples were shouting at each other. It was the age old concept of "you are responsible for this project failing." Sharon walked into the room and stood and waited. Finally someone realized that the pastor's wife was standing in the room watching their actions and listening to their immature conversation. Even though she was but 25 years old, she had always been mature beyond her years.

Finally she said, "I don't know what is going on or what the problem is, but the first thing I want us to do, before you tell me anything, is for us to get down on our knees and pray." They concurred, and all began to pray. She went from person to person, laid her hands on them, and prayed with each until they began to speak in tongues. One by one they dried their eyes and headed for the sanctuary. They may not have come to a conclusion about the subject at hand, but that was the last unmonitored Conqueror's meeting. The church was changing.

The allotted six-month period passed so very quickly. In fact, the elders and I were so busy that we almost forgot to execute an actual election of the pastor and have an installation service. During a Sunday afternoon meal at Jack and Marilyn Dawson's home, Sharon brought up the realization that it needed to be done. In a jubilant conversation about what the Lord was doing, Marilyn mentioned how time was flying by.

When they counted it up, Sharon said, "We have already been here seven months. Aren't we supposed to have some kind of an official business meeting about whether the church wants us to stay?"

Jack, who was the chairman of the elders said, "Oh, my goodness! I had completely forgotten about that."

Of course, arrangements were made, and District Superintendent Kitchen was contacted, so everything went off without a problem. Sharon and I were officially installed as pastor on Friday night, September 19, 1975. Superintendent Greene Kitchen (Sharon's father and mother), District Secretary Billy Cole, Sectional Presbyter Norman Mills, and my parents, Reverend James and Ruth Harper, were present.

One Sunday morning, Mary and Charles Lemley brought their boss, Doctor Chester Arents, to Sunday School to hear their new young pastor. He was the dean of the West Virginia University School of Engineering. (This man had been very ill the year before, and the Lemleys had arranged for their (then) Pastor Saffle to go to the hospital and have prayer for him. The man had credited that prayer with his recovery.) Before the morning service was over, he had calmly and sweetly received the baptism of the Holy Ghost. He asked to be baptized in water that night.

I walked into the baptistery, which was a concrete pool in the floor of the basement of the church. The water for the baptistery was from a spring under the church. The water constantly flowed through the pool at 54° Fahrenheit. When the tall Doctor Arents came into the water, dressed in white baptismal coveralls, with his black hair and black, horn-rimmed glasses, I realized that this was the man I told Sharon about in the dream I had while we were still at Dupo.

I said, "Doctor Arents, this is the second time I am going to baptize you. The first time I baptized you was in a dream I had while we were still living in Dupo, Illinois. You are a part of a confirmation of our divine destiny."

The growth began, and the demands for room to accommodate the people required resolution. Parking became the first priority. There was a huge elm tree next to the church that historically had been the sunny day picnic spot for various Sunday School classes. Once there had been only four classes to share it, but now there were eight because the pastor had given up his office space for another classroom. The elm tree had to go. It had lost its significance with growth, and beside this, it was taking up four good parking spots. All of the four additional lots that the church owned were graveled. Even still, the people were having to park on side streets. It was getting crowded and more classroom space was need-ed. Sharon related to me the story of the little brown house. It was a piece of property that sat across the street from their church in Huntington. It was pur-chased and converted to Sunday School rooms for the youth department. In Morgantown, there was no property to be bought close to the church, but the Frazier family did have apartments that they rented out in the basement of their home, which sat adjacent to the church parking lot. The church rented the two apartments and opened up six more classes. With the growth of the bus ministry, even more classrooms were needed. Two blocks from the church there was a 30' by 60' store building. In fact, this was the very building that Reverend H. I. Goodin and Reverend W. T. Poling had rented to start the Riverside Church. A trip to the courthouse revealed the own-ers. Jack Dawson and I contacted the owner and arranged to rent the building. It was remodeled and we installed folding partitions so the space doubled as an auxiliary function building and four more class-rooms.

One of the agreements that I had made with the congregation was concerning our compensation. Heretofore the pastors had taken 100% of the tithes and at times it had been difficult to cover normal expenses for the church. Sharon and I readily agreed that 20% of the tithing would go in to the church treasury to help maintain the cost of the operation of the church and 80% would be deposited into the ministerial account for me to take a paycheck and operate efforts of evangelism. Now that the church was growing, though, Sharon, because of her background, family, and training, felt very uncomfortable taking the amount of money that was coming to us as a result of the agreement. Without consulting anyone but the church treasurer, I instructed that a fixed amount be cut every week as a salary to Sharon and me and that the rest of the money be put into the church treasury. We knew that soon this congregation was going to need to build a new facility if this growth rate continued.

One of the women, Linda Kendall (who was working so hard helping her mother-in-law, Josephine Kendall, to raise money for the church projects) had not been able to yield her will to God while praying to receive the Holy Ghost. She had said that while she wanted the Holy Ghost, she did not want to lie on her back in the floor like others that she had seen. She wanted to receive the Spirit while just neatly kneeling in prayer.

After several services during which Linda almost surrendered to the Spirit and yet resisted losing control, Sharon said, "Linda, let's go back into the room where Brother Harper's office is, and you will get the Holy Ghost." When in the room with Linda and five other ladies, Sharon instructed Linda, "Now, no one is here but us. You go ahead and lie down in the floor, close your eyes, and start worshipping God with all of your heart." In a matter of moments Linda started to speak in tongues as God wonderfully filled her with the Holy Ghost.

I have the fond memory and pleasure of Sharon informing me that our little family was about to expand. This was a great consolation because just a couple of months earlier that hope had vanished when something went wrong and the hopes of a second child vanished. Now that it was a certainty the thoughts for a larger home transitioned to an absolute need that was inevitable. As back in Dupo, Sharon was the one that found the location for a new home. In light of the prices of homes 35 years later it is hard to imagine, but we were able to purchase a 3,000 square foot home plus two lots for $42,750.00 on Peach Street in the Marion Meadows subdivision of Morgantown.

The next Easter would see over 600 in attendance, and it became abundantly obvious that Riverside Apostolic Church was in need of a new address. Sharon suggested that a prayer chain be started with the sole goal of finding new property for the church.

She prepared a sign-up chart with spaces for the names across from the corresponding hours from midnight to midnight. The names were filled in, and the prayer chain focused on a new place for the church. One Sunday night, after several months of considering different properties, Sister Mayle stopped me in the small foyer of the church and told me about a location by the interstate that Coca-Cola had tried to purchase.

She said, "There are 25 acres at the Westover Exit for sale. For some reason Coca-Cola did not buy the property. I believe that this is the place for our church."

The next day, Norwood Dulin went with me to our friend, Judge Crynok, and asked him to help us locate the owners of the land. He reported back that he had located the owners, and that it was part of an estate with two-dozen heirs involved, and that they had just refused an offer from Coca-Cola of $50,000.00 for four acres.

The elders and the trustees met with me, and we decided to take the church financials to local banks to find out how much money we could generate to purchase the property. After the results of the request returned, the elders were surprised to find that I had been returning so much of the 80% of the tithing to the church. In fact, we had enough money that we could offer the heirs of the property $90,000.00 for the 25 acres.

Proper announcements were set forth by the trustees, giving the date of September 16, 1976, as the business meeting in which the congregation would officially decide if they wanted to purchase a new site and begin the journey of moving the location of the church. Sharon was expecting a baby. It would be our second child. When the date of the business meeting was set, it was two weeks before her due date. The morning of the business meeting, Sharon went into labor. I took her to Monongalia General Hospital and stayed with her until 6:45 PM. I came to the church. Everyone went into a tizzy because I was at the church while she was about to have a baby.

I told them, "Sharon said do what you have to do, God's got it all in control." To say the least, the timing of the arrival of this baby probably moved the business meeting along to the advantage of the church, because in only one hour, they made their decision to buy property and move the location of the church. They quickly sent me back to the hospital to be with Sharon.

As the time for delivery drew closer, I called Mama and Papa Kitchen and Grandma and Grandpa Harper. The Kitchens came immediately to Morgantown and stayed with Danielle at the house on Peach

Street. Early in the morning of September 17, Holly Renee Harper was being born. Then it got even more exciting.

As the nurse was applying pressure to finish the birthing process, Sharon screamed, "You're killing me!"

The doctor, a native of Italy, returned quickly to examine Sharon, and made the announcement, "Ole' my God, calls another doctor! There's another baby!" The delivery room became a frantic scurry.

I exclaimed, "Praise God, two more for Riverside!"

A second, unforeseen baby, a crash cart, a pediatrician, possible surgery for an emergency caesarian procedure, a PICC line, and "Oh, by the way, Reverend, you're going to have to step outside." Then 29 minutes later, without complications, Heather Dawn Harper was born. Other than the often-present infantile jaundice that kept Heather two days longer in the hospital, everything was wonderful—except that we now needed twice the baby paraphernalia than we had prepared for.

Sharon, AKA "Super Woman," was the mother of twin babies, the wife of a young, aggressive pastor, and was helping to undertake a building project that could kill a single, free woman, let alone one strapped with these multiplied responsibilities.

When I reported the results of the business meeting, the judge responded by telling me that there was no way that this amount of money would possibly buy this property. I insisted that he was obligated to at least present it. The judge thought that we would be laughed at. Three days later the judge excitedly called me and reported that the heirs said if the church would raise their offer to $100,000.00 that they would sell the 25 acres to the church! This was only the beginning of an incredible miracle of finance and provision for the Riverside Apostolic Church.

A title search was completed, a deed was prepared, and a schedule was set to circulate the deed to all of the heirs in 12 states from Florida to Oregon. Eventually all of the heirs had signed the deed except the one in Washington State. The courier with the documents arrived at the final heir's home at 3 PM. There was a great problem; he had dropped dead with a heart attack at 11:30 AM. Suddenly, there were 18 more heirs involved! I had just flown back in from a preaching engagement down south when the judge called to give me the shocking news. By a coincidence of divine timing, on that very flight home I had read an article in the airline magazine about exceptional estate considerations. The article had cited the Attorney General's office in Spokane, Washington, as having prepared a special release form for a family's executor to act in lieu of the deceased for execution of any business that was commonly known among the heirs within 48 hours of death. The judge said he had not heard of such, but he would contact Spokane. The next day the deed was on its way back to Morgantown, signed and notarized. The Riverside Apostolic Church had bought a new address on Dents Run Boulevard, just off the Westover Exit and within sight of Interstate 79.

The West Virginia District Pentecostal Conquerors, now known as the Youth Department, have an annual international fund drive called Sheaves for Christ. In 1976, if a church was able to raise $10,000.00 for SFC, the district sent that pastor and wife on a tour of Israel. Three churches had qualified: Valley Point Pentecostal Church, Staunton Street Apostolic Church, and Riverside. Holly and Heather were only six weeks old when it was time for the 10-day trip. Two factors weighed on Sharon. One was, "How am I going to go off and leave my babies?" and the second was, "I am so tired that I could use the break."

The Davisson family stepped up and said, "We will take care of your three girls." They had experience with twins. In fact, their youngest daughter, Jeannie, had given birth to two sets of twins, and the Davissons had had three different cows to deliver twin calves. They humorously claimed that the reason

Sharon had twin girls was she had visited the "Hidden Valley Farm" owned by the Davissons and had drank too much of that creek water. The girls went out there for the duration of the trip. To help know who was who, Sharon painted Holly's big toenail red so she wouldn't get them confused when she got home.

Several other church members joined us on the trip. It gave Sharon and her parents a wonderful opportunity to be together, which was especially nice because their time to visit had been very limited ever since she had left for Texas nine years earlier.

The church was at full bore, with a course charted that demanded work, strategic planning, and money to enable all to see the dream come to life. Sharon watched me stay up late at night as I personally drew the plans and created a set of working prints for the development and construction of the new facility. In spite of the fact that she was raising three little girls, two of which, as you know, were identical twins now just under a year old, Sharon set out to get the job done to help raise the money. Remember, she was only 25 years of age when we moved to Morgantown. The tradition of the church was that you had to be at least 36 to join the Ladies Auxiliary at the church. Since she was the pastor's wife they made an exception and let her join.

There is such a thing as doing too much too soon. I have always been a pusher. The Morgantown Mall was having an anniversary celebration. Having heard of it, I went to the mall management and volunteered the church choir to be featured during the anniversary functions. Of course, I believed that my wife should attend everything that I did. After consulting with the choir leaders, I found that they were not comfortable with such a grandstand presentation. I asked if they would consider it if I got them some help. They agreed to give it a go, so I contacted my friend, Jim Stark, who had worked for years with Hugh Rose and the church at Jewett, Ohio. After one of the choir practices, Sharon and I, the twin babies, Danielle, and Jim went out to eat. Being the gentleman that he is, he immediately started helping Sharon with the baby carriers while I parked the car.

As dinner progressed, Jim got to thinking about him being single and having gone to all of this effort carrying around babies and the paraphernalia, and so he interrupted the flow of conversation and said, "Sister, I'll help you as much as you need, but if you ever tell this, I'll swear you're lying." Everyone broke into a roar of laughter.

After going home that evening Sharon told me that she was so tired that she didn't think she could go on without some help. She could tell that at first I thought she was being stubborn or even rebellious about the music, church program, and schedule. Yet after some genuine pouring out and openness on her part, I realized that the strongest part of my ministry was about to collapse if some exceptions were not made and made quickly. We contacted Sharon's parents and arrangements were made to meet in Flatwoods, West Virginia, which was ideally halfway between Huntington and Morgantown.

The choir outing at the mall with Jim Stark was a major success. The rest for Sharon did her a world of good, and the education for me about overtaxing people was probably one of the best lessons I ever learned. You see, I had an excellent instructor—the one person who loved me more than anyone in the world, my wife, Sharon Kay Kitchen Harper.

Three major things were about to happen, of which two would become annual events, and the third would be ongoing. One was a fall festival, for which we rented the entire Riverside Junior High School for three days and set up shops in every room. It was like a craft mall where you could find pottery, ceramics, wood crafts, quilts, pepperoni rolls, baked goods, clothing, furniture, and, of course, a spaghetti dinner. The results of that first effort produced nearly $10,000.00. It also revealed an incredible leader, Sharon Harper.

The other events were the annual rummage sale and auction, and the weekly pepperoni roll production by Gram Kendall, which continued to crank out funds for the building project.

Now it was one thing to get excited about building a new church, but it was even more important to keep the spiritual intensity of the church at a revival level. Sharon was always my biggest fan, but there were some things that she realized that I could not do. In her submissive fashion, she asked if she could have the women of the church to meet with her at 5 PM on the first Sunday of every month to have what she called "Ladies Growth and Worship." Out of those sessions came great revival, and a host of unsaved husbands that rallied around me and began to join the volunteer labor force at the new property. Sharon began to teach a series of Bible studies on family lifestyle and successful marriage practices that resulted in the parade of faith, with the women of the church who were married to unsaved husbands marching around the church complex and declaring that the unbelieving husbands would be saved by the sanctified life of the believing wife. Almost all of those husbands, numbering over 25, either are in the church or were and have gone on to Glory.

On the first Saturday in February, 1978, I led a group of men into two feet of snow at the new property site. Armed with chain saws and axes we started clearing the property. On every Saturday at noon for the next five years, unless there was a wedding or funeral, Sharon organized the women to provide a meal for the men who were working on the new church project.

The many people that made the Riverside dream come true may be too numerous to attempt to tell; however, there were a few outstanding incidents that happened in the development and building of the Dents Run Facility that were nothing less than a God thing.

One of the young girls at the church had been selected as the Homecoming Queen at her high school. She had a lot of natural beauty, intelligence, and talent. She was asked to represent the school at the state level in the West Virginia High School Homecoming Queen competition. As that young lady's sister put it, "We all knew there would be no contest. Why, she's the prettiest person that I know." Sure enough, Diana won the state crown. The rules stated that in order for her to go to the nationals she needed a non-family member as a chaperone. Because of the love of the family for Sharon, they unanimously insisted that she be Diana's chaperone to Las Vegas, Nevada.

It was there that Sharon not only shined as an Apostolic but also, with kindness, impacted several lives and welded lifelong friendships. On more than one occasion she guided the family group around some undesirable situations. At one time during dinner at a famous hotel venue, the lights came up on the stage area and they announced Joan Rivers. After the applause, the entertainer made the usual thank-you comments and then spewed out a string of obscenities; Sharon stood up, walked from person to person in the party, and quietly led them all out of the room. One among the group, a grandmother who was not associated with Apostolic convictions, commented that Sharon may have been only 28, but she was a real mother of strength and godly principles that was not afraid to be who and what she was anywhere that she was.

Chapter 12
Speak to the Mountain

The biggest physical obstacle on the new property was a mountainside. As you may know, there are so many mountains and valleys in West Virginia that if the state were flattened out it would be bigger than Texas. To create the building site and prepare the land to handle the 40,000 square feet of building and the necessary parking, over 500,000 cubic yards of earth was going to have to be moved. I had contacted several earth-moving/mountaintop coal-moving companies to give the church bids on how much it was going to cost to move the mountain. The bids came in and ranged from $600,000.00 to 2.5 million dollars to move the earth and to do the site prep work. After reading the four bid letters, I was in deep despair. Sharon came into the kitchen of our home where I was staring out the window in deep thought. When she laid her hand on my shoulder giving an affectionate squeeze, I didn't respond in my usual adoring manner to her.

"Tell me what's on your mind," she said.

"Oh," I began, "I have been so sure that all of this building has been the perfect will of God and now I feel like Moses at the Red Sea. I have a people following me, and I've got this huge mountain in front of me with not enough financial resources to get it done. I've got one more bidder coming this afternoon, and I know he's going to be too high even before I get there."

Her words are still clear in my mind.

She said, "This doesn't belong to us. This is the work of God, and He has always provided for His people. I've seen it all of my life in the things Daddy did in Huntington. You go talk to the contractor, and I will go pray."

Folks called the contractor "Big Jim" because he drove a gold-and-black GMC Gentleman Jim pickup truck. He always smoked a big cigar. He walked back and forth across the property with me, and stopped beside his truck (which was parked beside a stack of logs that were ready to go to a local sawmill that had bought them).

He said, "Preacher boy, I'm going to do you folks a real favor. I'll move all of this for $375,000.00."

I responded, "I don't think that we can afford that. Can you do it for less money?"

"No, but I'll tell you what. You holy-rollers preach out of that book that with faith as a grain of mustard seed you can speak to the mountain and move it. If you get this done for less, you're going to have to talk real loud to this one." Then he bellowed and laughed.

I shuddered, turned toward the mountain, and at the top of my voice screamed, "God, I am not going to be intimidated by this cigar-sucking sinner. In the name of Jesus Christ: mountain, be thou removed, and go anywhere else but here!" I turned to the man and thanked him for the inspiration.

Big Jim said, "This is going to be fun. Nobody will believe what I just saw. If that's the way you move it, this mountain side will be here a long, long time."

I invited him to church and bid him another thank you.

That was Friday evening. When I got home Sharon told me that she had a good session of prayer and wondered how things had gone. I was about to tell her "not so good"—but I never got to finish my sentence because the telephone rang.

The voice on the other end said, "Reverend, did your church buy that piece of property over on Dents Run Boulevard where they are cutting down all of the trees?"

"Yes," I replied.

"This is Captain Larry See of the United States

Army Reserves 1092nd Engineer Battalion. We are looking for a place to do some training maneuvers, and we were wondering if your church would let us practice there and move some dirt around for you."

There were other people that got involved such as Bobby Donham, Rocky Marko, Ernie Riley and his uncle's H-977 high lift, the WV Department of Highways, Leonard Lewis and lots of men from the church. One lady came to Sharon on a Sunday morning and said, "My husband doesn't believe that there is enough room on the property to keep all of the earth here and wanted to know if he could help by hauling some of it away?"

Sharon brought Shirley Buzzo over to me and told her to, "Tell Brother Harper what Frank had said." The next Saturday, Frank had his brothers and sons there with their big coal trucks and Ernie Riley, Bob England and myself took turns for several weeks loading hundreds of trucks and watching God *move the mountain.*

Big Jim stopped by for a little while every day and watched the mountain disappear. His bid cost: $375,000.00. *God's cost: $10,000.00.*

Those 25 acres had been bought for $100,000.00. The Ladies efforts and the returned tithing allowed the church to purchase the property and build a beautiful 50' X 100' colonial fellowship hall that was furnished with a commercial kitchen and an evangelist quarters.

While the construction of the fellowship hall was taking place, I engaged an evangelist to conduct a protracted meeting. It lasted for two weeks. Sharon was the one who stayed at the house, fixed three meals a day, changed all the beds, and planned all the social functions for the guest as well as took care of a six-year-old and a set of two-year-old twins. With all due consideration, Sharon had planned an outing and thought that it would be good for me to join in on the Monday night rest day, to go to Pittsburgh and fellowship with her and the evangelist and his wife. The plan was I would get up early, go to the construction site, get things started, and be back by 10 AM to leave. To get right to the point, when I went that morning there was only one man working, a mason. He had no help. I got involved in helping. 10 AM turned into 2 PM, and Sharon, without cell phones in those days, got in the car and drove over to the building. Well, the evening was almost ruined, but it was salvaged only because Sharon was a lady filled with grace. She absolutely protected me from any possible whim of conflict. This was a reflection of the tremendous tutoring she had received from her mother.

A local businessman saw the development of the

area and paid the church $100,000.00 for four acres. At a later time, another two acres were sold for $50,000.00, and two other sales netted the church $100,000.00 more.

As of this writing, the Riverside Apostolic Church is utilizing five acres that, in essence, cost them nothing.

The decision was made to start the transition from 110 Monongahela Avenue to Dents Run. September 9, 1979 the fellowship hall was finished and the first service was held in the building. It was used as a transition facility for three and one half years.

The decision was made to keep the Sunday School at the Monongahela Avenue site and move the Nursery and the Adult department to the new building at Dents Run that was capable of seating 400 people. The rented auxiliary building was discontinued as the old church and the fellowship hall could accommodate the attendance. The buses of the bus ministry were utilized to keep the congregation from feeling that they were separated. The buses took the children to the old facility for the 10 AM service and delivered everyone from Monongahela Avenue to Dents Run at 11:30 AM. Sunday, Tuesday, and Thursday night services were conducted at the fellowship hall.

As the church was settling into the routine of services in two different locations on Sunday mornings, Sharon and I felt that it would be good to bring some assistance to the church to help administer the rapid growth that was being experienced. Because of their longtime relation with the Coles of Parkersburg, West Virginia, we were very familiar with Jack Cunningham, the son of Hilda Cole Cunningham and the grandson of the late J. C. and Mary Cole. Jack had just married his Colombian bride, Elsy, and he was preaching around in some revival meetings when we asked them to come and assist us in Morgantown. Jack and Elsy arrived on Saturday, November 3, 1979.

Sunday was their first services with us. Monday, while Elsy and Sharon got to know each other better, I took Jack all over town and introduced him to everyone with whom the church conducted business. We went over the business plan of the church and registered Jack as a resident member of the clergy at the surrounding hospitals. Tuesday was a day of meeting the local community leaders and giving Jack several church growth books that would familiarize him with my philosophy about revival and church structure.

Tuesday, November 6, 1979, at 7:30 PM the Bible study service began. There was a great liberty in the worship that night, and everyone was excited about the presence of the Cunninghams deciding to come to Morgantown. At the appropriate time, I came to the pulpit and announced that I was going to use the Scripture and prove that Jesus Christ indeed was the Mighty God, Jehovah, and 359 Bible verses later, the congregation was on its feet in worship as nine new souls were filled with the baptism of the Holy Ghost. Sharon looked up from the music that she was playing and watched me dancing before the Lord in worship. She closed her eyes and continued to play. When she opened her eyes again, she saw me kneeling in an odd fashion beside my seat on the platform. She would later describe my complexion as a pale shade of green, as I was struggling to right myself and get into a chair. She rushed over to me.

She shouted, "Baby, baby what is wrong?"

With an already paralyzed faced, I struggled to get my mouth to form the words, "I think I've had a stroke."

She motioned for help. Jack asked the church to pray, and someone placed a 911 call. A church member named Delmar Walker, our friend since we were teenagers at camp and who was also a local Morgantown fireman, said, "Get him in my car, I'll have him to the hospital before the ambulance can get here."

At the church, Brother Higgins Donham challenged the church to "not let the sound of prayer cease" until their pastor walked back into the pulpit to preach again. Reverend Jack Cunningham quickly organized an around-the-clock prayer chain at the church and then joined us at the hospital.

During the ride to the hospital, I was able to communicate to Sharon that I was not going to die.

I told Sharon, "This is the bruising that the prophecy was about."

Chapter 13
Divine Intervention, and a Miracle

The prophecy had come earlier in the year while I had been preaching the youth camp at the Oklahoma District. During the last night of the camp, an elderly lady had come up onto the platform.

The lady meekly had approached me and said, "I've never ever done this before, but the Lord just spoke this scripture to me, and He said that I needed to share it with you. It is Isaiah 53:10: 'Yet it pleased the Lord to bruise him; he hath put him in grief: when thou shalt make his soul an offering for sin, he shall see his seed, he shall prolong his days, and the pleasure of the Lord shall prosper in his hand.' You are going to get very ill, but you will recover, and God is going to use you to cause His Kingdom to prosper. Brother Harper, I will be praying for you."

During the same service, only a few minutes later, Reverend Roy Moss, the Youth president of Oklahoma, came over to me and related how that throughout the preaching that night the Lord continued to impressed upon him to share Isaiah 53:10 with me.

Brother Moss said, "I am not sure what this means, but the Lord assured me that you will know."

In the month following that youth camp, Reverend Billy Cole had come to Morgantown. He had with him a dear friend, Reverend Chaiyong Wattanachat, superintendent of the United Pentecostal Church for the nation of Thailand, who was in the USA for a visit. I had taken them to breakfast at Lakeview Country Club and Inn. After breakfast, as we got in the car to go to the church, Brother Chaiyong prophesied ominously.

In his broken English, Chaiyong said, "Brother Harper, you are going to be used of God in a different way. It pleases God to get glory through you by allowing you to almost die and then giving you a testimony to convince many that you are chosen of God to minister to them in the Holy Ghost and His gifts."

I asked, "When will this happen?"

Billy Cole answered, "You will know. Today is a confirmation to reinforce your faith when your trial comes."

◆ ◆ ◆ ◆ ◆

So, in some of my last conscious moments I said to Sharon again, "This is the bruising. I am not going to die."

This odyssey of faith moved from the church to General Hospital, where the initial opinion was that this trauma should be blamed on a local fast food restaurant, due to a rash of food poisonings that had been associated with it. Without a diagnosis, I was moved to the West Virginia University Hospital. In about an hour the emergency room physician, along with Dr. Stephen Cooper, then doing a neurology fellowship with Dr. Nugent, asked Sharon to come into the family consultation room. In no uncertain tones he told her that I had suffered a severe hemorrhage.

He stated simply, "A blood vessel has ruptured in the outer surface of your husband's brain, and he is profusely bleeding into the cranial space that holds the brain. The area outside and around his brain is filling with blood so fast that it is threatening to crush his brain. Nine out of ten patients die within 12 hours. If he lives until morning, we will do an arterial-gram to see just where the hemorrhage is located. Now if he should survive for a week and we are able to do surgery, seven out of ten patients die in surgery. If he lives beyond that, he will be permanently impaired in one form or another. If you have family, you need to get in touch with them, because you are going to need all the support that you can have available to you."

Stunned at what she had just been told, staggering under the weight of this information, this incredible rock of strength wrapped her arms of faith around the words "This is the bruising. I am not going to die." Holding on for three little girls and the life of the love of her life, she outwardly remained in control. She stayed at the hospital throughout the night, and she was there when Doctor Cooper came in.

The doctor said, "Mrs. Harper, your husband will probably die today, however we are going to do the arterial-gram, and hopefully, since he is in such good physical health, he will survive that."

I survived the test, but this brought more gloom, because the bleed was confirmed to be every bit as bad as had been projected. Immediately they began a series of lumbar punctures (spinal taps) to draw the excess blood out of the spinal cord to relieve the pressure on and around the brain. They moved me from the emergency room area into a neurology room on the fourth floor. The windows were all blackened, and the lights were turned down. Orders were given to Sharon and the family to not make any noise or conversation to stimulate my brain, because I needed total rest if I was to survive at all.

Sharon's mother and father, along with other families and friends, had now arrived from Huntington. Sherry Dulin had made arrangements with compassionate church members to take care of Danielle, Holly, and Heather so Sharon could go home and rest. When Sherry got Sharon to the Peach Street home, kindly but strongly, Sharon said she just wanted to go into the house by herself. Once she was inside and heard the car pull away, she threw herself down across the first steps of our split-foyer home and began to wail and sob and cry out to God. She had to believe that her husband, a man of God, knew what he was talking about. She kept remind herself by telling God, "This is the bruising. I am not going to die."

Jack Cunningham summed it up the best when said, "Sharon Harper is an incredible lady." He made it clear with, "I have been in and around ministers' and pastors' homes all of my life. When Brother Harper brought me here and introduced me as a preacher, his wife instantly treated me as if I were a seasoned veteran. I had always been used to being treated as though I was still a child and did not know what I was doing. The amazing thing about Sister Harper was that she empowered me to do the job that the pastor had brought me here to do." And it was so. He took care of managing the church services, the visitation of people who were also ill at home or in the hospital, and the coordinating of activities in and around the church. Since Jack was present, then the thing to do was to help and not hinder the dream that had inspired me to bring the Cunninghams to Morgantown—that of making the church grow.

One of Sharon's close friends was shocked when Sunday rolled around and Sharon made plans to take the girls and be at church instead of being at the hospital with her sick husband.

To the shocked expression Sharon responded, "I'm going to both church services today because that is exactly what Edwin would ask of me."

Sure enough, come Sunday—even though I have no recollection of it—I began to talk. I had asked if they had all gone to church, who was there and wasn't there, and I asked Sharon to bring Jack in. What I did not realize was that Sharon had almost never left my bedside. In the darkened room there was one small nightlight to help the folks get around without falling. Sharon had sat at that light and crocheted by the hours, to pass the time and pray. Her hands were busy, but her spirit and mind were in touch with God. When she had left to go home, whether going from or returning to the hospital, she would go to the church and pray. The sound of prayer became somewhat famous for this time of need, and people had driven hundreds of miles just to be a part of the continuous prayer meeting. Jack had been there every day. When Jack came into the room, I started telling him who needed to be visited, who needed to be called, and even gave him the phone numbers from memory—yet to this day I don't remember any of those things. Seventeen days are forever gone from my memory.

November 23, 1975, is the first day that I remember. I faintly recalled telling the nurse to call Sharon and tell her to bring me clean underwear. (Later I found out that I had asked for those items every morning since I had been in the hospital.) Later that day the fog cleared, and standing at my bedside was Sister Mable Boster, who had come to Morgantown to help Sharon with the girls, along with Mabel's daughter, Ruth, who was married to Sharon's brother, David. In just a moment, Sharon arrived. Immediately she noted a keen difference in me, and she asked for the nurse to come to the room.

Doctor Stephen Cooper was called. Sharon commented on more than one occasion that she had learned to identify the sound of his footsteps coming down the polished, tiled hallway. She hated that sound, because every day that he had come to check on me he had never left the room without telling her that I would probably die that day. Deep down inside, she knew it would be different today. Every day the nurses had done a lumbar puncture and drawn out spinal fluid. Sharon had watched the procedure daily, and she noted that the fluid, which on prior days had been a deep red color, was now a faint pink. She realized that the brain was not bleeding. Doctor Cooper ordered another puncture. The fluid was clear.

"Well, Mrs. Harper," he said, "your husband is going to live. We are scheduling another arterial-gram for Monday, so that we can get an exact location of the bleed and go in and surgically close the void in the ruptured blood vessel."

The nurses came into the room and removed all of the light-blocking materials from the windows. Doctors, interns, and medical school students filed in and out of my room for the next several days. The phrase "he's probably going to die today" had gone away.

The radiology lab was administered by Doctor Bill Noble, who happened to be my next-door neighbor. Joining him in the lab were Doctors Nugent, Fox, and Cooper. The procedure for an arterial-gram is much the same as for a heart catheterization, except that the heart is by-passed in the routing of the catheter, and it is moved up the carotid artery and into the blood vessels of the brain. Typically a contrast agent is injected. A series of radiographs is taken as the contrast agent spreads through the brain's arterial system, then a second series as it reaches the venous system of the matter that surrounds the brain and spinal cord. I had been unconscious during the first procedure. Today, I was fully awake.

The first angiogram was performed on November 7, 1979, the morning after I had been rushed to the hospital. A video tape had been made of that procedure. As the second procedure got under way, Doctor Noble got the catheter in place while the other three reviewed the video of November 7. Doctor Fox, the neurosurgeon, directed the catheter to the blood vessel that the video showed the contrast agent gushing from out into the cranium. He released the dye. I was so glad I knew nothing about the first test, because immediately the pain was excruciating. However, there was no resulting leak as had showed up on the previous test. The doctor moved to a corresponding vessel and released another load of dye. There was plenty of pain, but no leakage.

The doctor revisited both blood vessels once more (for each) and then Doctor Nugent said, "This man isn't going to need surgery, someone else has already been here."

Alice Stansberry, a member of Riverside Apostolic Church, was the nurse in radiology that day. She was standing behind the team of physicians. When she heard Doctor Nugent's statement, she threw her hands in the air, spun around like a top, and started speaking in tongues.

Dr. Noble said, "Alice, what are you doing?"

Alice replied, "Doctors, this man is my pastor and I've just witnessed a miracle." Those words—"a miracle"—would stick.

Doctor Cooper came up to the room. He spoke with Sharon about the type of activities allowable for me for the next few days at home, and he signed the discharge papers for her to take me home with her. They wanted me to return in one week for an outpatient test called a myleogram.

I returned and went through the test. It was worse than the other tests, and I suffered a headache for three days following the test. The good news was that there was nothing wrong in the subarachnoid tissue around the spinal cord. Doctor Stephen Cooper came to my room as Sharon and I were gathering up our articles in preparation to exit the hospital.

"Mister," he began, "you are the luckiest man that I have ever met. When you came through these hospital doors you had three out of a hundred chances to survive this episode—even after surgery. You are a medical phenomenon; you have a total recovery without surgery. All of your karma was working for you."

I said, "Let me share this with you. I received the baptism of the Holy Ghost and was baptized in the name of the Lord Jesus Christ when I was 11 years old. This lady here experienced the same when she was 10. I started preaching this gospel when I was 14 years old, and I have been faithful to God all of my life, as she has also. The church that we pastor has not been without the sound of someone praying since this happened to me. What you have witnessed is the miracle-working power of God."

Doctor Cooper responded with, "I don't know anything about your God and Ghosts, but I will admit that the only explanation that we have for your case is divine intervention. You are a miracle."

With that, they closed the three volumes of my records (which were each four inches thick) with the words, "Divine intervention, and a miracle," signed: Doctor Stephen Cooper.

Chapter 14
Realization of a Dream

Sharon was a patient woman. Even though the ordeal that she had just come through with me had resulted in a victory, there were some emotional difficulties that I had to deal with that created some challenges for Sharon in caring for the children. In the process of recovery we discovered that I became agitated and restless much quicker.

Once I retorted, "You hated every minute you spent at that hospital with me."

Sharon hid her frustration and said, "No, I didn't, but tell me, did you not want me there for some reason?"

"Oh, I wanted you there. I just feel like I have put you through so much that you must be tired of me."

Tearfully Sharon answered, "I am tired, but not of you. I am just so glad to have you alive and well in my world. You are the love of my life."

Sharon scheduled her life and the life of the family to accommodate the church, my preaching schedule, and the entertainment of guests—all while carefully protecting me and our girls from any unnecessary confrontations.

In confidence she said to an old friend, "My job is to make sure that he is always seen as the wonderful husband, father, and pastor that he really is. If we are to have a good life, then this is my assignment."

"Blessed are the peacemakers."

The regaining of strength after having lain still in a bed for twenty-six days presented a mild challenge. However, in due time everything slowly returned to near normal. During this period, Sharon's mother and father made several trips from Huntington to Morgantown to assist with the children and help Sharon in any way possible. As recoveries go, I finally decided that I felt strong enough to go to the Mountaineer Mall and walk around. Brother Kitchen volunteered to drive me over to the mall. On the way over, in his soft voice, he began to give me some obvious advice.

"You know, Brother Harper," he said, "your body is somewhat like a tire. After you run it and run it, sooner or later a weak spot develops and the tire gives out. In your case the weak spot that developed was your head." We had a good laugh as Brother Kitchen tried to fix the faux pas, but every comment just made it worse. Today Sharon occasionally reminds me that I have a weakness "in the head."

◆◆◆◆◆

I was finally strong enough to return to the church. For the first few services, Sharon had set me in a special chair on the main floor to just observe and enjoy the choir and the preaching of Brother Jack Cunningham. The delightful discovery was that, during the time of illness and recuperation, God was working a phenomenal transformation in the church. They had learned the power of focused prayer. It is noted that during the 26 days while I was in the hospital, God had used this powerful prayer time to empower the church and the ministry to advance the efforts of soul winning. Brother Cunningham had baptized 26 new families in the name of the Lord Jesus Christ, and God had filled them with the Holy Ghost during that time. Brother Cunningham and his wife, Elsy, reiterated that the demeanor and attitude that Sharon demonstrated throughout this whole ordeal gave them room to grow into their own and be confident about the special ministry for which God was preparing them.

By January of 1980, I was back in the full swing of the role of pastor. The Cunninghams were invited to go to Chicago to assist Pastor Mike Anderson. With our blessings and a generous love offering raised by Sharon, they were able to move to the next opportunity in life without feeling financially challenged.

♦ ♦ ♦ ♦ ♦

The next year was not without incident. This would be our first Easter of dealing with the split locations. The annual Gold and Blue attendance campaign produced another record attendance for the Sunday School with almost 800 in attendance. Sharon and the women of the church began to plan a huge Spring Festival using the convenience of the new address to its fullest extent. A bake sale, craft show, quilting rack, and, of course, a dinner were all parts of the agenda for the Memorial Day weekend.

Moving onto the grounds of the new address had created quite a lot of excitement. My miraculous recovery and the continuing addition of new converts had stirred the hearts even more. The inevitable suddenly became obvious: the main sanctuary and educational facilities must be constructed to move the whole operation to Dents Run and accommodate the growth of the church.

That year the annual district conference would be held in Beckley, West Virginia, and the General Superintendent of the United Pentecostal Church International, Reverend Nathaniel A. Urshan, would be the presiding officer of the conference. Sharon and I had been associated with the Urshan family as respected acquaintances since our time in Dupo, Illinois. At this particular conference, it was my lot to be the evening devotional leader and Sharon was the organist. Brother Urshan took note of our familiarity with all of the old Pentecostal hymns. He asked us to be the devotional leaders at the annual General Conference (a huge, international meeting of the UPCI) that was scheduled for Philadelphia in October.

Following May, we were off to youth camp at Point Pleasant, West Virginia. At that time the youth population of the district's churches demanded three weeks of camp to handle all of the campers. At the conclusion of the camp, as we were loading our car to return home, a neighbor called and told us that our house on Peach Street was flooded. After the two-and-one-half-hour trip to Morgantown, during which we were filled with dread, we arrived home to find that sometime after we had left the prior Monday, a washer hose had burst. Water had sprayed from it for the entire week. Terry Lewis, the general contractor that had built our home, was building across the street, and he was using electricity from our house. When his helper had gone up Friday to unhook the electric cable, there was water running out from under the garage door. Terry had managed to get into my SUV and had used the garage door opener.

Terry said, "Reverend, I know what the Red Sea looked like to Pharaoh. When I put the door up, water rushed out—a foot deep. Inside, all of the upstairs floors are soaked, and your ceilings are all ruined downstairs."

A resident from down the street came by while we were standing out in the street, surveying the damages. He was there because he came to tell on our eight-year-old, Danielle, for beating up on his little boy the prior Tuesday. He said he had been watching for us to get back because he wasn't going to tolerate his child being bullied. Sharon's intestinal fortitude was again revealed.

She, knowing that there yet remained some frailty in her husband's body, stepped between the man and me and said, "Edwin, I can see that he's made you angry; don't you say a word. Remember, you're the pastor of that church, and they don't need you getting out of line." Then she turned to the man and said, "Mister, you're way out of line. First of all, right now we are stressed to the max because of this mess here at the house. Second, my husband is still recovering from a serious illness, and, thirdly, you don't know what you're talking about, because Danielle has been at camp and at my parent's house for three weeks, and it is impossible for her to have been here and beat up on your pipsqueak son. Your safest bet is to get on down the street while you can on your own power." Needless to say, Mama Lion wasn't to be messed with, and so he disappeared. It was never mentioned again.

We had already spent three weeks in a motel room with the girls at camp. Seven additional weeks and $23,000.00+ later, we were able to move back into our home.

General Conference in Philadelphia came and went. The focus in Morgantown was on gathering finances to build the balance of the church facility.

After the General Conference, Reverend Kenneth Haney invited us to be his guests at the annual fund-raising conference for Christian Life College, an event called "Landmark." I was one of the evening speakers. Before we left the hotel that evening, we went down to the restaurant for an evening meal. The three girls were dressed so nicely. Sharon had this awesome green velvet, three-piece, matching outfit on. Her hair was up in the traditional Pente-costal style, and we had just sat down for a relaxing time before church. The waitress approached the table, coming up behind Sharon. Suddenly, the tray she was carrying—with five glasses of water and a pitcher of water—shifted. The waitress tried to re-cover, but to no avail. At least a gallon of water poured out, with almost all of it going onto Sharon's hair, shoulders and back. Other than a drop or two, at the most, that splashed on me, Sharon had the coldest shower of her life at the table. Outthinking everyone in her family, she politely got up, graciously accepted the waitress's apologies, refused her offer to pay the dry cleaning bill, told me and the girls to go ahead and order, and that she would be back. Obviously she went without supper. However in about the length of time that it takes to do a restaurant meal and pay the tab she returned with an altered hairdo and a different outfit. Later that evening, she was telling Reverend and Mrs. Haney about the experience. Brother Haney commented that he did not know very many people that would have handled it so calmly.

To that Sharon replied, "What choice did I have? My husband was preaching tonight, and I was not going to let anything upset him or distract him from the message that he was about to offer."

Sister Haney said, "Now that is a God-called minister's wife."

I assured them that she had always put the ministry and the work of God first.

Later that week, at the close of a powerful service, we had gotten down between the pews to pray, in responding to the closing comments of the message. While we were praying, I looked up at Sharon and told her that I knew how to get the money to start the work to build the church and education facility at Riverside.

"What are you going to do?" asked Sharon.

"I was just impressed to see if Wilbur Hemann would like to move his construction company office to Dents Run Road."

The time at Landmark was so wonderful. Sharon so enjoyed the time she was able to spend at the Haney's ranch. Their home was a beautiful, colonial style house with all of the signature décor of the cattle boon era of California.

As soon as we returned to West Virginia, Sharon expanded the incredible program she called "Growth and Worship." In lieu of the former concept of a "Ladies Auxiliary," Sharon believed that since the women of the Lord's earthly life were the first to carry His "Resurrection Message," that it was significant for them to choose the better part of sitting at the feet of Jesus as well as the domestic duty of dinner and silence. "Growth and Worship" was a monthly meeting of all of the women and daughters of the church, coming together on a set Sunday at 5:30 PM for praise, prayer and scriptural inspiration. Their worship in the sanctuary set the stage for the Sunday night service, at a Holy Ghost fever pitch that, without fail, paved the way for God to pour Himself out on the whole congregation throughout the evening. These services were such a part of Sharon that when we would move to Huntington, this model became the standard of the Staunton Street Apostolic Church, which paved the way to a 300+ soul revival in 1988.

While Sharon was leading the women, I would be working with the men as we moved closer to the groundbreaking for the church and educational complex on Dents Run. I also followed through on the answer given from God earlier—I talked to Wilbur Hemann, the owner of Commercial Builders. Wilbur had married the granddaughter of Sister Bliss, a longtime member of Riverside Apostolic Church.

Wilbur Hemann had previously declared, "Since I have been attending church with Judy, I have found a new sense of direction, listening to the singing and preaching of Brother and Sister Harper. I feel that I can help make a difference in this city by helping them."

Remembering that statement, I approached Wilbur and asked if he would be available to give a bid on drying in the new facility. I gave Wilbur a set of blueprints, detailed like the sets I had given to two other building contractors elsewhere, and I asked Wilbur to give the church a price on foundation, concrete floors, masonry walls, roof structure, and concrete-and-steel second-level floors, balcony, and stairways, for the 27,000 square foot facility. Wilbur came back with a bid of $100,000.00, which was less (by between $35,000.00 to $45,000.00) than the other two contractors. The elders and I reported to Wilbur that he had given us the best price.

I explained my idea to Sharon. I confessed that it might sound ridiculous, but that I was going to ask Wilbur if it was possible to trade some land for building supplies and labor. With Sharon's support I proceeded. I met Wilbur for breakfast. I explained that the location of the property was so convenient to the interstate, and, with the tremendous amount of excavation that had been done to create level land, that the east end of the property would make a great place to headquarter Commercial Builders. Wilbur confessed that he needed more space, and he asked me what I had in mind. I asked how much land C. B. would need. With his answer of approximately four acres, I produced a copy of the land transaction that I had secured, concerning the location across the interstate from Dents Run, where Coca-Cola had finally bought. They had paid $65,000.00 for 3.5 hillside acres—which still had to be leveled. Being influenced by my father and father-in-law, I knew that it was easier to negotiate down rather than up.

"Look here, Will," I began, "Coke paid over $18,500.00 per acre for land they had to level before they could get started. As you figure every day, excavation is expensive. To you, is an acre of ground that is level worth $30,000.00?"

"Well," he said with a pause, realizing that this young preacher had put him on the spot, "yes, but it should go down in price if I buy more than one acre."

"Ok," I answered, "What is it worth if you end up with four level acres with interstate access and a self-advertising location?"

"Boy, you're tough," he said—this not being his first land negotiation. "I'll give the church 22 an acre."

"Tell you what," I answered, "I've got the bid with me that you made to the church to build the new sanctuary. I know that you have some profit margin in your bid above the material and labor. Without writing a check to the church, give us a finished project that matches the bid, and a release of any and all liens, and you will only have to lay out of pocket about $78,000.00, make your margin of profit, and take ownership of the four acres after the bid specs are met, and we will show on the deed that you bought it for $100,000.00."

"Well, I guess I just bought four acres. Make it $25,000.00 an acre. We got a deal."

When the initial phase of the building was complete, I went armed with the blueprints, the release of liens, and the church financials, and I started out from bank to bank, making the case to borrow the balance needed to finish the work. I had a commitment from three banks. The big challenge now was interest rates. First National Bank of Morgantown met our need.

Just as we were about to complete the facility, Keith Hemann, Wilbur's oldest son, who had been the construction chief on the buildings, fell 40 feet to his death while on a jobsite in Kingwood, West Virginia. He had hit headfirst on a concrete floor. His father was so moved with love for his son and the church, that he furnished the finances to cover the total cost of all of the foyer area of the church, in memory of Keith.

During the time of construction, two poverty-stricken mothers, each with a little baby girl, came to Sharon separately and presented her with the sad news that they could no longer give adequate care to the children. Sharon contacted an attorney and asked what steps were necessary to assist the young mothers in finding help. At that time the state agencies that today offer food, medical assistance and clothing vouchers were not as accessible as they are now. The attorney gave her definite directions and told her to be on the lookout for prospective adopters. This odyssey allowed her twice to experience both the ridiculous and the sublime, as she was the custodian of the court that was charged with the responsibility of having an infant given heartbreakingly to her by the birth mother and joyfully delivering the child to waiting and excited adoptive parents.

The church was in need of $100,000.00 to complete the sanctuary and move into it. Bill Buzzo brought us that amount of money—plus $53.00—inside two Quaker State Oil boxes. The money was held together in stacks by rubber bands. When it was taken to the bank to be counted, the dust and mold plumed out of it every time that they opened another stack. Almost all of the money was in $1.00 bills.

With arduous labor, the building was completed, and the first service was held on Easter Sunday, April 3, 1983. The attendance that day was 1,001, a new record for the church. The following year would see the record broken again, with 1,107. That set a new record not only for the church but for the United Pentecostal Churches in West Virginia, as well.

The Ladies Growth and Worship, nursery care program, the Sunday night choir, the youth choir, the "Hallelujah Chorus" (the Sunday morning choir for members 55 and older) and the social interactions of the church all felt the constant influence of Sharon. Every Sunday at 7:00 PM she directed the church, as it would record a 30-minute radio program that would be aired the following Sunday morning on

WCLG, 1300 on the AM dial.

There is no way to record all of the great and small contributions that we shared to make the 10½ years in Morgantown, WV, such a monumental success.

Chapter 15
Not the Easiest Mountain To Climb

For about five years, Sharon's father had been talking about the possibility of us leaving Morgantown and coming to Huntington to assume the responsibilities of the Staunton Street Apostolic Church where Sharon had been raised and where we had been married. In fact, when the children would visit with their grandparents, Brother Kitchen would purposely teach them a little rhyme he coined: "Come on people, let's all cheer. Away with Morgantown, we like it down here." At first they were reluctant, but eventually, because they wanted to please him and have his delightful approval, they readily chimed in, and he would respond with his hearty laugh and fun-filled facial gestures. We both felt that we would spend our entire lives in Morgantown. I had gone as far as to acquire cemetery spaces there, following the admonition of Reverend J. T. Pugh, who had said, "No pastor can be effective if he doesn't plan on spending a lifetime there." Repeatedly, we would respond to the suggestion (that we would be in Huntington) with a loving decline and a forward-sighted statement about the future of the Riverside Church. Brother Kitchen eventually confessed that he had given up all hope for us to make such a transition when the move to the Dents Run property was completed.

April 30, 1985, was the 35th Pastoral Anniversary for Reverend and Mrs. Greene Kitchen at the Staunton Street Apostolic Church. Sharon and I had worked diligently to arrange for the services. We had engaged Reverend and Mrs. Nathaniel Urshan, General Superintendent for the United Pentecostal Church International, to be their guest speakers for the anniversary. It was a four-day affair that reached into May. On the last night of the services, I had accompanied Brother Kitchen to the Gateway Holiday Inn to pick up the Urshans and drive them to the evening service.

While we were waiting outside of the hotel in Brother Kitchen's 1984 Ford luxury van, Brother Kitchen looked at me and said, "Brother Harper, I have to talk to you about this before you folks leave to go back to Morgantown. You and Sharon have always seemed very reluctant to discuss the possibility of you folks coming to Huntington and becoming the pastors of this church. I don't want you to interrupt me. Let me finish talking, and then you can have a few days to talk with Sharon about it. I am going to be retiring. I have been looking around, and I do have some other unsure options. Someone is going to follow me here, and it would be better for the whole family if that someone were you and Sharon. I know that there are challenges, but I also feel that it is the will of God."

About that time, the Urshans came out the door, and with Brother Kitchen's gift of perfect timing, the answer and response from me was put on hold—to simmer in my spirit until the next morning. When church was over, and Sharon and I were alone in our room at the Kitchen's home, I related the posed suggestion to Sharon. There wasn't a dash of consideration.

Sharon responded, "Why, I don't think that there is any way that could work out." Morning was coming, and Brother Kitchen was going to pursue the conversation.

Nothing of it was said during breakfast. Brother Kitchen said it would be good for me to accompany him in taking the Urshans to the airport. I did. On the way to the hotel to pick them up, he began his banter about the dream of old men being canceled when young men put their ambitions ahead of the will of God.

He would say things such as, "Do you have any idea how many pastors have spent a lifetime at a church and then have to leave the love of their life and go off somewhere else and not be able to attend and enjoy the continued growth and blessings of their work?" On he went, all the way to the hotel. He never gave me a chance to reply, and then it was time to stop talking about the subject because guests were in the van. The conversation shifted, and until the Urshans got on the plane, it was all about them. Then, once we were back in the van for the 20-minute drive back to the house, the conversation got redirected to the church. I was going to get to talk.

I returned to the conversation by informing Brother Kitchen that Sharon and I had talked about the transition, and that we had come to the conclusion, for several very personal reasons, that we did not think it could work. Being the insistent soul that he was, Brother Kitchen pursued by challenging the idea that it could not work out, stating that anything can be worked out if it is the will of God. He further pressed for an explanation as to why it would not be feasible.

I responded with, "I think you and Sharon need to have a private conversation."

Later that day, Brother Kitchen made it a point to interact with his youngest daughter. He listened to her explain some family and in-law challenges from her childhood days.

He simply said, "I think we can work through it." Then he offered a sense of perspective by adding, "You see, the will of God is not always the easiest mountain to climb."

When Sharon was able to speak to me again, in her tongue-in-cheek fashion she said, "Do you want me to kill you? Why did you tell Daddy that we needed to have a private conversation?"

"First of all," I responded, "he is your Daddy, and he needed to hear any real reasons for hesitating about a move back to Huntington from you and not me."

You must remember that, at the time, the church in Morgantown had become the largest UPCI church in West Virginia. As she often says, "I felt like their mother, because over 70% of the church had received the Holy Ghost under our ministry."

Also bear in mind some of the considerations she has observed, such as, "Going back to Huntington was returning me to the position of the pastor's daughter and not the pastor's wife."

Nevertheless, she said that if a thing proved to be the will of God, she would not hesitate to be obedient to the Lord.

Brother Kitchen and I talked about the transition

in more detail later that day. Brother Kitchen insisted that it was the will of God. I told him that I needed to know for sure that it is the will of God.

I said, "Sharon and I have a piece of property on the Grafton Road. We are getting ready to build a new house there. Let me tell you what I am proposing to God. If my house sells, which is up for sale, we will know that we are to stay in Morgantown. If the property on Grafton Road were to sell, which is not up for sale, we will know that it is God's will for us to come to Huntington."

Saturday afternoon, Sharon and I headed back to Morgantown. On Sunday the services at the Riverside Church were excellent as always. It felt like Morgantown would always be our home.

Monday morning I took our car to the Exxon station in Westover to get an oil change. Next door to the station was the Westover pizza shop. It was a favorite for the locals, and rightly so, as the food was so delicious. I walked over, sat down, and ordered a sub sandwich and Coca-Cola. Just as my order arrived at the table, Johnny Marco came in. He was a coal operator and county politician. I had a great relationship with most everyone in town, so Johnny felt comfortable to come over and join me at my table. The following conversation took on meaning that would change our lives forever.

"Preacher, got any more land for sale?" Johnny began while picking up the menu and motioning for the waitress.

"Oh, I got a really nice home I would like to sell you."

"If you sell your home what are you going to do about a house for you guys?"

"Sharon and I have 2½ acres out on Grafton Road. We thought we would build us a new home there."

In his forceful fashion Johnny insisted, "When you are finished eating I want to drive out there and take a look at your property."

"OK, I've got my car next door, and it will take them a while to get it done. I'd love for you to see it." It took about fifteen minutes to arrive at the property. Looking over the level ground, a rare commodity in Morgantown, WV, Johnny had nothing but admiration for the site.

As we were about to pull off and start back to Westover, Johnny spoke up and asked, "What would it take to buy this piece of land?"

I almost swallowed my tongue, because selling this property without advertising or telling anyone that it was for sale was the fleece that I had made public to Brother Kitchen, to confirm that it was the perfect will of God for Sharon and me to resign the

Riverside Apostolic Church and move to Huntington to become the pastors of the Staunton Street Apostolic Church. With great thought, I looked at Johnny and gave him a price. It was a price that, if Johnny wanted that piece of property badly enough, would pay for Sharon and me a new home in Huntington.

"Reverend, would you really sell it to me for that price?"

"Yes, I will."

Johnny stopped his black Grand Cherokee, put it in park, and opened the glove compartment. He pulled out his checkbook, and wrote me a check— on the spot—for the whole amount.

He said, "Hold onto this check until the abstract is complete on this place, and then deposit it in the bank. You are making my family very happy." Johnny would go on to build a 1.5-million-dollar home on that plot of ground. When I got back to my car, I went straight home and told Sharon. She could hardly catch her breath.

She said, "I was afraid that this would happen. Edwin, are you sure you didn't try to sell this to Johnny?"

"Sharon, I tried to sell him our house."

I called Brother Kitchen to tell him what had happened. As you read, bear in mind that this was before the days of "Caller ID."

When he answered the phone, Brother Kitchen immediately said, "Well, Edwin, who bought the Grafton Road property?"

"How did you know it was me?" I responded.

Brother Kitchen said, "I have heard from God."

The next month was filled with emotional swings for Sharon and me. When we informed our oldest daughter, Danielle, she was absolutely thrilled. We did not mention it to Holly and Heather until we were in the car, headed for Huntington to try and identify either a home or a lot to build on. Just a few miles out of Morgantown, Sharon began to explain to them what was going on. The twins became so upset that I had to pull off the road and park so that the girls could be consoled. It was the longest drive we had ever made to Huntington.

Sharon and her mother set out to look at some properties. The thought and the thrill of a new home helped her overcome some of the agony of dealing with the complaints of the twins as well as the depression of leaving the Riverside family. Within the month, we had settled on a lot in a relatively new subdivision. I had taken on the task of a set of prints for the construction and setting in order what had to be done to make this happen.

Once the house was dried in, we took off for Hawaii for ten days. Upon returning, I worked tirelessly, and I was able to move our family into the new home after 122 working days.

In the middle of the building of the house, the church in Huntington conducted a formal business meeting and officially made us their new pastors alongside Brother Kitchen.

Sharon, with the blessing of her father, began to be more than the pastor's daughter. For many years, he had directed the church choir. Sharon assumed those duties, and the excitement of a new day—along with her special talents—created almost immediate growth in the choir. Within the year, it was necessary to remodel the platform to make room for new members. The church attendance began to increase, and it was not long until it was necessary for the choir to remain in the choir loft throughout the service. Brother Kitchen was absolutely thrilled with the growth.

For years, the record Easter attendance at the church had been 1,026. This record was set back in 1973. As many people knew, the church in Morgantown had set the new state record of 1,107 in 1984. Now that we were in Huntington, everyone wanted to return the Staunton Street Apostolic Church to the #1 spot in Sunday School attendance. In a Sunday morning service that featured the choir, plans were executed and a push was made to fill the new gymnasium on Easter morning, 1986. It was a success, and Brother Kitchen was so elated, as Sunday School had been his secret for building a great church through the years. A record number of people, 1,056, came to church that Easter morning in Huntington. The choir sang, and Brother Kitchen preached to the largest crowd ever assembled in an Apostolic church in West Virginia. After church, the family was assembled at a buffet in South Point, Ohio. Candidly, Brother Kitchen sat down beside Sharon and whispered, "Everything is working just fine. Thank you for coming to Huntington."

Here is a side note (bear it in mind for later): In a matter of days, Brother Urshan, General Superintendent of the United Pentecostal Church International, contacted me and said he wanted me to consider pastoring a large church in the Midwest.

One thing led to another, and before long Sharon was conducting a "Growth and Worship" service once a month for the ladies of the Staunton Street Apostolic Church. Each time, the thrill of the ladies service would spill over into the Sunday evening evangelistic service. Excitement was running high. The women were rallying around Sharon. They were soon planning trips to ladies conferences and special ladies retreats in different states. The atmosphere in the church was very healthy.

The one area of struggle was with the domination of the music by Sister Harper's older sister. You see, she had been playing either the piano or organ at the church since 1950. As you might realize, Sharon and I had been ministering together as a team for the past 20 years. When I would go to the pulpit to preach, the older sister made no effort at all to give place for Sharon to play in support of me. It was not that she had never allowed a minister's wife to accompany their husband. In fact, it was her normal practice to leave the organ bench so that a visiting minister's wife could come to the organ if she played for him in a service. Sharon spoke to me and asked how much longer it would be before we could function as we always had before returning to Huntington. At first I said we would just be patient. I then eventually realized that we had been in Huntington for over two years, and she hadn't offered to give room for Sharon. I remembered that the pianist (who had been playing music way back on the night that Brother Kitchen had received the Holy Ghost), had said to Sharon that her time had arrived and that it would only be right for her to start taking care of the song services. Just playing music in the church service was not the issue. Having the right songs ready before I preached, and having the appropriate music for the close of a good evangelistic service after the sermon, were of the utmost importance. In fact, once after I had preached a stirring message to bring the church to a moment of consecration, I had seen the fire put out when the older sister started to play "His Eye is On the Sparrow." I later asked her why she had chosen that song.

She had responded, "It sounds pretty, and I like to play it."

The time had come for Sharon to play. When I came to the pulpit the following Sunday, I asked for Sharon to help me at the organ. The older sister began to cry. She jumped up and ran out. The end results were that Sharon's brother and nephew also put down their instruments and joined her exit, commenting that if the older sister wasn't good enough to play for Edwin, then neither were they.

Sharon approached her Dad and asked what was going on. He immediately called for the big sister to come over to the house and sit down and talk. She did. She told them it was simply the fact that Edwin didn't want her to play the organ. Sharon spoke up and informed her that the only reason that Edwin had asked to have Sharon at the organ was because Sharon had insisted that a change happen.

Sharon said, "You have no idea how nervous that had made Edwin. In fact, he wanted to wait, but I insisted."

Big sister said, "Well, why didn't you tell me yourself?"

"I had, but you didn't respond."

"Oh," she replied and said nothing else.

Sharon continued, "What about Bubbie?" That was the siblings' name for her brother, David.

"You ask him."

Sibling rivalries take strange turns. Bubbie's response to Sharon's inquiry was very direct.

He said, "I always wanted Edwin to be the pastor of this church, but I don't want you to pastor. I want him to." With that, he stopped coming to church, and unfortunately so did his son, Davey. (Remember David and Davey. They both will be back later in the story, in the next book.)

It certainly was an interesting setting at that point. The influence that the older sister was now about to wield on Brother Kitchen was incredible. For years, whenever she could not get her way, she reverted to tears and the claim that all of her life she had been cheated. Her marriage was less than good, her health certainly was poor, her weight was out of control, and she was very depressed. The fact that Sharon and I had moved in on all of them was just more than she could handle. It became obvious that some manipulation was happening. For years she had exerted her control of the church through her father. Now the church was on the move in a major way, and she was out of control. So, it was time to play the tears-and-feel-sorry-for-me card. There was a certain trip that Brother and Sister Kitchen had taken on a regular basis for several years. Each summer, they would go to Gatlinburg and enjoy a time of getting away. It was not uncommon for them to invite family members that were available, and not working, to go along. This year, as a consolation to the sister, she was invited to come along. During the trip she poured out to her "Daddy" how that the church was just being taken away from them and how that Edwin was disrespecting Daddy.

When they returned, Daddy called me to come to his house for a talk. The conversation was short and direct.

He stated, "You have moved in and just taken over everything."

I responded by rehearsing the history of how it was that we were now living in Huntington. At that moment, the elder was so emotionally distraught that he called me a liar. Highly insulted and confused, I left the house. I told Sharon what had just taken place.

She said, "Well, I guess Charlotte has finally gotten through to Daddy how unhappy she is." Sharon revisited a three-year-old conversation, and, without saying 'I told you so,' she reminded me that she didn't think it would work. Simply said, sibling rivalries and jealousy have even wrecked empires.

As painful as surgery is, there are times that it is the only answer to a problem. Sharon and I simply decided not to go back to the Kitchen house. Later that day, the mother and father came over to our home, but I met them in the driveway and explained that Sharon was not ready to talk to them.

Several days passed. The phone rang. I answered it, and Brother Urshan told me that Brother Kitchen had called and expressed that he had made a big mistake, and that communication had ceased and he needed to apologize for the situation that he had allowed to develop. Brother Urshan insisted that I call my father-in-law immediately and hear him out. Out of respect for the General Superintendent, I submitted and made the call. Brother Kitchen asked if he could come over and talk.

I said, "Let me see if Sharon is up to it." Her answer was yes. In a few minutes he was at the door. Strained-but-kind exchanges were given. Coming into the home, Brother Kitchen apologized for his accusations, and said he wanted to know why Sharon had not been returning his phone calls. With that I welcomed him to the living room and went to bring

Sharon into her father's presence. For two hours they sat privately in the parlor and spoke frankly to one another.

At one point Brother Kitchen said, "So you see that's how it is."

With a bit of her father's wisdom, she answered his conclusion with, "Yes, Daddy, I am sure that as honest as you are, to you that is exactly how it is. But let me be just as honest and explain to you how it is to me from where Edwin and I are living."

For some time she related some very personal challenges that involved another extended family member. She went into detail and reminded him of the plea and the agreed offer that he had made them to lure them to Huntington. Point by point she peeled back the onion of their lives and shared some intimate emotions. She covered the fact that they had no intention of taking anything away from him, her mother, sister or brother. The agreement to come to the church was to enhance him and the rest of the family. One statement that she made was echoed by him several times before he left this world in 1994:

"Edwin and I didn't come here to Huntington because we didn't have a work to do for God. My husband resigned as a member of the district board, left a community where the business people and civic leaders begged him to stay, resigned the largest church in the state, and humbled himself to be your subordinate until you decide to retire. It is not fair that you act as if we came to run over you or the family. In fact, in the last three years you are the pastor of the largest congregation and Sunday School in West Virginia." At this point I came back into the room.

Brother Kitchen said, "I will resign and leave."

To this I responded, "Not a chance. If anyone resigns and leaves it will be me. You see, I am not about to live under the banner that I disgraced an elder, especially my father-in-law. Either I leave, or we both stay together. We did not agree to come back here for you to leave. We came back so you could live out your life enjoying the church and congregation that you built. You have several grandchildren, and three of them are my children that eventually I will have to pastor. If they feel I ran you off, I will never be able to help them make heaven. I have to live with me, and someday I, too, will be ready to face what you are facing."

At this time Sharon joined in and said, "Daddy, we are here because the church has to be bigger than the family. You raised me that way." Brother Kitchen thanked Sharon and me for our courtesy and said that Minnie was waiting for him to come home.

Only a few moments after he left the house, Sharon said, "Edwin, I just would like to go sit on my Daddy's lap and hug his neck."

I responded, "Why don't you just call and see if it would be OK to come over there?"

"What if they don't want me to bother them?"

Encouraging her, I said, "Oh, don't worry. They are always going to be Mommy and Daddy."

She immediately picked up the phone and Sister Kitchen anxiously said, "Please come over."

It was a better-than-pleasant visit. During the visit, Sister Kitchen revealed where she had always been in the process. "I told Greene he better not get wrapped up in all this complaining Charlotte Ann had made on the trip. I told him, 'You've gone to a whole lot of trouble to get Sharon and Edwin to come down here, and made a lot of promises.' I told him he had better live up to them, because Edwin can go anywhere in America and pastor. He doesn't have to stay here and take this treatment and pressure."

Sharon just hugged her mother without making a comment.

Chapter 16
This Pain is Different

The following Tuesday, Brother Kitchen made the announcement that he was formally retiring on the anniversary of him being elected as pastor of the church back in 1950. With that, he introduced me. (He always called me, "Brother Harper.")

He announced, "Brother Harper and Sharon are now the Pastor and First Lady of the Staunton Street Apostolic Church." It was amazing that the discussions and family resolutions were kept to the family. Over the years this had been a trademark of the family—that family privacy must always be honored.

I refused to just take over. It was my feeling that this was not an agreement between us men, but this had to be a choice of the congregation. A formal business meeting was properly announced and held, and the congregation voted. As a matter of fact, by then the congregation was twice as large as had voted on the original proposal for me to join Brother Kitchen as pastor. They voted almost unanimously (with an exception of only seven ballots), to officially, by election, declare me as the pastor of the church. In that meeting, Brother Kitchen was officially named "Pastor Emeritus."

Immediate plans were formulated to host a retirement week, and the transition of pastors in a formal matter. A week was devoted to the celebration of Brother Kitchen's pastorate. Throughout that week, his retirement pension from the church, a benefits package, a brand new 1989 Cadillac, and a brand new 1990 custom Ford van for travel, were all presented to him.

The mayor came and gave him the "Key to the City of Huntington"—a gesture that had never before been extended to a resident.

At the banquet to honor this great couple, Brother Kitchen said, "I never dreamed a man could be so honored in this life."

It was necessary to build a new sanctuary to accommodate the growth that had preceded the transition. Once emotions relaxed, Sharon and I began to consider what would be the appropriate approach to solve the seating problems that were being encountered even in the gymnasium, where folding chairs were set up to accommodate 200 more on Sunday night than the 1967 "Cedar Sanctuary" could hold. Following the lead of the families' dear friend, Brother Kenneth Haney, we drove Brother and Sister

Kitchen around Huntington and considered several optional building sites. After some talk, it was decided that rather than to duplicate all of the buildings and property that was already owned by the church, it would be wisest to make the investment right where they were on Staunton Street.

Within weeks we had a set of prints to present to Brother Kitchen. The reader may wonder why, if I was the pastor, we were asking the former pastor's opinion. In spite of the fact that Brother Kitchen had turned everything over to us, it was obvious that a giant such as Brother Kitchen knew something about successful planning and pastoring. Many years prior we had learned that you do not become pastor of a congregation overnight. In fact, an elder had shared this secret: "It takes seven years of service to become pastor. You have to preach that many funerals, dedicate that many babies, and marry that many couples, as well as laugh and cry with that many families, to be called that pastor. Until then, you are a guest preacher serving until the hearts of the people make you pastor." We decided there would be no chance granted for any folks to think the former pastor was being slighted.

The only change he asked of us was that a suite of offices be added to the plans and that I make sure the exterior complement the existing structures. With that some changes were made. Sharon worked out the interior and decorations.

When the plans, ever so detailed, were presented to the city, the building inspector refused the prints because I was not a licensed architect. $23,000.00 later, and with a congregation ready to move, the inspector again refused the plan because the building was too tall, too long, and too wide. At this point the mayor, whom Sharon and I had befriended, got involved. The building is there today as a silent testimony of the power of friendship. That same mayor became a regular in Sunday School.

Using the good relation that Brother Kitchen had built with the banking community, financing swiftly was put in place.

We were joined in the groundbreaking ceremony by Governor Gaston Caperton (a real fan of Sharon), Mayor Bobby Nelson, the bankers, and several other city, county, and state officials. One year and 17 days later, the governor was back for the opening service on November 4, 1990. In May of the following year, the West Virginia District conference came to the Cathedral, and Rev. N. A. Urshan, the General Superintendent of the United Pentecostal Church International, came and dedicated the facility.

Brother Kitchen continued to teach his Bible class on Sunday mornings until he was physically unable to do that. He was always the master of ceremonies for all Sunday night services and for the 8:00-to-9:00 PM Sunday radio program, "Live From The Cathedral." Sharon made sure that every request and whim of her father's was met.

As the Cathedral was completed, the very first office completed and furnished was the one that Pastor Emeritus Kitchen would occupy. Sharon decorated it with all of his memorabilia from 44 years of pastoring. It was a favorite room to visit, because there was always an explanation to go along with all the pictures and awards.

In October of 1993, Sharon's father felt severe pain in his abdomen. He was a 70% disabled veteran of World War II. He was not a stranger to pain. Throughout his life he had health issues that always threatened to sideline him. In 1955, two-thirds of his stomach had to be removed due to ulcers. He had fought hepatitis, heart attacks, pancreatitis, and bypass heart surgery. Yet, as he related to Sharon, "This pain is different." In mid-September he went to the V.A. hospital for tests. The results were due to come back the Monday after the UPCI General Conference in Louisville, Kentucky. As an honorary member of that General Board, he always looked forward to the fellowship of his ministerial comrades. With great joy he attended the conference. He returned home and went to the V.A. for his report.

When he returned, he gathered the children to-gether and gave them the bleak news that he had a large, cancerous tumor growing in his stomach. The following week, his youngest grandson, Marc Kitch-en, was scheduled to be married in Farmington, New Mexico.

Without any thought, he climbed on the plane and made the trip. He came home from that grand occasion to enter St. Mary's Hospital in Huntington for the surgery. It was a touching ordeal to say the least. For weeks he was hospitalized. Several times he was just a breath from death. Sharon made it a point to just be there. Finally he was able to come home.

As they were getting things together for the trip home, a doctor came to his room and said, "Mr. Kitchen, we have found that your cancer has spread to your liver. There is nothing else we can do for you. You probably have six months to live. Get your af-fairs in order."

Brother Kitchen called his wife and requested that all of the children come to his room. As they came in, he greeted each and gave them the report. Then Sharon heard her Dad set the parameter for the final charge.

"Now don't overreact," he declared. "We are the children of God, and we are going to face this just like we have faced every other challenge; trusting the will of God."

To that Sharon replied, "Daddy, you are the bravest person I have ever known."

Once home from the hospital, every effort was made to assist in recovery. Every day Sharon and her siblings were at the house, taking turns assisting their mother and serving their father. There was a time that it looked as though recovery was in the making for Brother Kitchen, but he kept assuring Sister Kitchen that he knew his destiny, and that she must prepare the children for the inevitable. As soon as he was able to eat and swallow some food, Sharon cooked and carried to her father anything he thought he might want. He insisted that life be carried on through Christmas as though nothing was wrong. On his 75th birthday, January 13, Sharon organized a "This is Your Life" service at the church. He was not able to attend, but through the telephone he was able to listen in and hear all of the wonderful stories that the church and friends had to share with him. A highlight of the evening was the presence of longtime campground companion, Rev. Daniel Coleman.

Sharon contacted his many minister friends and asked them to come to the house and see him. Along about March, he seemed to get stronger. Sharon asked her Daddy if he felt like preaching again.

To this he replied, "Yes, I have a message the church really needs to hear."

On "Family Day," during the Easter attendance campaign, he came out on a Sunday night and preached "Choked Wells," challenging every member to clear the way for the waters of the Holy Ghost to freely flow in their lives.

He preached, "All of us have a date with destiny, and you must not allow anything to prevent you from joyously leaving this world and being gathered to Jesus Christ." He returned home and deteriorated quickly. Sharon asked her Dad if there was anywhere special that he would like to go by taking a car ride. He said, "Boy, that is a hard question. I love the old home place in Webbville, Kentucky, and you know how much I love the campground in Point Pleasant, West Virginia." After some thought, he chose the old home place. A week later, David was able to take him to the campground. That would be the last place he would ever visit.

It was a very uplifting day, and the spirits of the family were high. It seemed that Brother Kitchen had rallied, and he was in good spirits. He seemed so much stronger. He had Sister Kitchen to call the children and their spouses because he wanted to talk and visit with them. When they got to the house, he had already asked for David to come to his bedside, and then his wife. Soon Charlotte and Tommy were invited in. Not long after that, he asked for Sharon and then me. Today would be different, because for the first time in thirty years, he addressed me as Edwin. Each child and spouse received specific instructions about their future and their relationship with God, the church, and Sister Kitchen. Finally, he told us all that he was tired and excused us so he could take a nap.

The next day began with anxiousness, because Brother Kitchen was noticeably weaker. Sharon was at the house all night, along with David and Charlotte. Charlotte had left for a while to get some rest. David had lain down in the back bedroom. Sharon was with the nurse, and her cousin, Wanda, at her Daddy's side. As he expressed discomfort, Sharon was praying.

Suddenly he said, "Well, it's all alright. Don't pray for me to get well."

Sharon said, "Daddy, I am only praying for the will of God. That is the way you taught us. You told us God can do anything, and I believe He is able to raise you up whole, but I know God has a plan."

A few moments later, he drew one breath and relaxed. At that point, Sharon raised her hands in worship, and she began to speak in tongues as her Daddy met Jesus face to face.

Pastor Greene Kitchen, who was born January 13, 1919, passed from this life to Glory on April 20, 1994. He had fulfilled his divinely inspired path in this earthly life. Sharon and I continued on toward the fulfillment of ours, while living in a glass house called the parsonage.

To be continued
in the next book.

Made in the USA
Charleston, SC
15 October 2015